# THE *Change* OF *Conversion* AND THE *Origin* OF *Christendom*

# Christian Mission and Modern Culture

EDITED BY
ALAN NEELY, H. WAYNE PIPKIN,
AND WILBERT R. SHENK

In the Series:

# THE *Change* OF *Conversion* AND THE *Origin* OF *Christendom*

ALAN KREIDER

TRINITY PRESS
INTERNATIONAL
HARRISBURG, PENNSYLVANIA

Trinity Press International, P.O. Box 1321, Harrisburg, PA 17105

Trinity Press International is a division of The Morehouse Group.

Cover design: Brian Preuss

**Library of Congress Cataloging-in-Publication Data**

Kreider, Alan, 1941–
    The change of conversion and the origin of Christendom / Alan Kreider.
        p. cm. — (Christian mission and modern culture)
        Includes bibliographical references.
        ISBN 1-56338-298-9   (pbk. : alk. paper)
        1. Conversion—Christianity.   I. Title.   II. Series.
BV4916.K74    1999
248.2'4'09015—dc21

                         99–40924
                            CIP

*Printed in the United States of America*
99  00  01  02  03  04  6  5  4  3  2  1

In memory of
John S. Oyer
(1925–1998):

Mentor, Model, Friend

# Contents

# Preface to the Series

Both Christian mission and modern culture, widely regarded as antagonists, are in crisis. The emergence of the modern mission movement in the early nineteenth century cannot be understood apart from the rise of technocratic society. Now, at the end of the twentieth century, both modern culture and Christian mission face an uncertain future.

One of the developments integral to modernity was the way the role of religion in culture was redefined. Whereas religion had played an authoritative role in the culture of Christendom, modern culture was highly critical of religion and increasingly secular in its assumptions. A sustained effort was made to banish religion to the backwaters of modern culture.

The decade of the 1980s witnessed further momentous developments on the geopolitical front with the collapse of communism. In the aftermath of the breakup of the system of power blocs that dominated international relations for a generation, it is clear that religion has survived even if its institutionalization has undergone deep change and its future forms are unclear. Secularism continues to oppose religion, while technology has emerged as a major source of power and authority in modern culture. Both confront Christian faith with fundamental questions.

The purpose of this series is to probe these developments from a variety of angles with a view to helping the church understand its missional responsibility to a culture in crisis. One important resource is the church's experience of two centuries of cross-cultural mission that has reshaped the church into a global Christian *ecumene*. The focus of our inquiry will be the church in modern culture. The series (1) examines modern/postmodern culture from a missional point of view; (2) develops the theological agenda that the church in modern culture must address in order to recover its own integrity; and (3) tests fresh conceptualizations of the nature and mission of the church as it engages modern culture. In other words, these volumes are intended to be a forum where conventional assumptions can be challenged and alternative formulations explored.

This series is a project authorized by the Institute of Mennonite Studies, research agency of the Associated Mennonite Biblical Seminary, and supported by a generous grant from the Pew Charitable Trusts.

*Editorial Committee*

ALAN NEELY
H. WAYNE PIPKIN
WILBERT R. SHENK

I welcome this discussion of Christendom. As an American who for three decades has lived in England, I have sensed that we will not fully understand the current malaise of Western Christianity until we come to terms with the phenomenon of Christendom in its many dimensions. Our Christian past shapes our Christian present; decisions taken in the past shape our current predicaments and possibilities. And yet, although many people recognize this, there has been little attempt to define Christendom as a term or to discuss it systematically as a phenomenon.

In this volume I will try to present a brief taxonomy of Christendom. My thesis will be that insight into the distinguishing characteristics of Christendom can come through studying the means of conversion that were used to produce it. In this, I am following a hint by the eminent American church historian of fifty years ago, Kenneth Scott Latourette. At the beginning of the first volume of his epic *History of the Expansion of Christianity,* Latourette pondered this question: "How far may medieval and modern Europe be ascribed to the methods employed in the conversion of its people?" (1944:xv). Latourette did not answer this question, nor will I do justice to it in this brief book. But I hope that what I have written can point the way forward for further discussion of the issue.

In what follows, I will attempt three things. First, in an attempt to distill the essence of conversion in the early centuries of the church, I will tell stories of early Christian converts and examine the processes by which they became Christian. Other scholars have preceded—and accompanied—me in this interest. All scholars have viewed conversion in the ancient world as an aspect of change; etymologically, *epistrepho, metanoia, conversio* all connote change. But scholars' interests have concentrated on differing dimensions of this change. Kurt Aland and Arthur Darby Nock were above all concerned with beliefs; for the former, conversion was "the change of belief," whereas the latter saw conversion as the "reorientation of the soul of the individual" (Aland 1961; Nock 1933:7). To this, Wayne Meeks has added a special attentiveness to belonging; for him the corporate dimensions of conversion—"the resocialization into an alternative community"—are especially important (1993:26). Ramsay MacMullen's studies have, in contrast, concentrated on the experiential dimension of conversion—especially the encounter of potential converts with supernatural power (1983). Thomas Finn, in keeping with current initiatory programs in the Roman Catholic Church, has placed central emphasis upon the ritual dimensions of conversion (1997). And William Harmless, in a remarkable study of Augustine's approach to conversion in its early Christian context, has discussed a "journey of conversion [that] is lifelong, communal, and required of all" (1995:362).

As I proceed in this book, I will draw appreciatively upon the work of all these scholars; to some of them I am considerably in debt. They have pointed to important aspects of the story that must figure in any overall treatment of conversion. But I will want to add my own emphases. As I read the records of the early Christians, I am struck by the way in which conversion involved change not just of belief but also of belonging and behavior. Scholars writing on early Christian conversion have at times referred in quite general terms to this. Note this recent sample: "the task of conversion was to reshape an entire way of living and system of values" (Finn 1990:609). But often scholars have not given due weight to these dimensions, so that when they tell the stories—some of them very famous—of early Christian converts they overlook the concern for ethics and solidarity that, to me, is evident in the texts. I want to bring this concern into responsible focus within an overall understanding of conversion that involves a process of multidimensional change. As I see it, in Christianity's early centuries conversion involved changes in belief, belonging, and behavior—in the context of an experience of God that, for all the reticence of early Christian witnesses, for some people must have been very powerful.[1]

Second, I will attempt to chronicle the changing nature of conversion. As the centuries went by and as Christians gained influence and the capacity to induce and compel adherence, the content and configurations of conversion altered. Familiar words remained in the Christian vocabulary; traditional rites continued to be performed. Belief, belonging, behavior, accompanied by experience—all of these continued to be parts of a shifting package of elements. But the relationship of the parts within the package changed. As we will see, Caesarius, mid–sixth-century bishop of the city of Arles in Gaul, urged people to a conversion that was different from the conversion that Justin of Rome had experienced in the mid–second century. In these four hundred years a new Western Christian civilization—Christendom—had dawned, and conversion, which entailed change, had itself changed.

Third, I will look at Christendom. I think it is significant that this word—so central to the history of the West—has been used so freely and with so little thought as to its meaning. In this era of Christendom's disintegration, we need to be a bit more thoughtful about the character and inner dynamics of Christendom. As I have worked, I have sensed that Latourette's hunch is correct, and that the characteristics of the Christianity of the West can be clarified when examined in light of the methods of conversion that produced it. So I will look at Christendom under the categories of belief, belonging, and behavior. I will also suggest learnings from early Christian conversion that I believe query models that are popular today, and I will propose alternative forms of Christian thought and praxis for the future.

When I was an undergraduate in the 1960s, I read Sir Herbert Butterfield's *Christianity and History*. At first reading, this book made a powerful impression on me, and some passages from the book have continued to resound in my consciousness. One in particular was important to me when, in the late 1980s, I was considering shifting research areas from the English Reformation to early Christianity. In the following passage, Butterfield—a Methodist lay preacher who was to become Regius Professor of Modern History at

Cambridge—suggested an approach to Christianity's past that I decided I wanted to explore. If Butterfield is right, the study of the past can provide direction for its future.

> After a period of fifteen hundred years or so we can just about begin to say that at last no man is now a Christian because of government compulsion, or because it is the way to procure favor at court, or because it is necessary to qualify for public office, or because public opinion demands conformity, or because he would lose customers if he did not go to church, or even because habit and intellectual indolence keep the mind in the appointed groove. This fact makes the present day the most important and the most exhilarating period in the history of Christianity for fifteen hundred years; and the removal of so many kinds of inducement and compulsion makes nonsense of any argument based on the decline in the number of professing Christians in the twentieth century. We are back for the first time in something like the earliest centuries of Christianity, and those early centuries afford some relevant clues to the kind of attitude to adopt (1949:135).

As I have worked on this book I have been aware of being at an intersection between the historical study of early Christianity and the missiological task of thinking about mission in contemporary culture. I have found it personally rewarding at this intersection to try to bring some order to the flows and blockages of traffic. If as a result of my work "the earliest centuries" can open us to "some relevant clues" for Christian mission in modern culture, I will in part have repaid my long-standing debt to Butterfield—and will be very grateful.

I would like to thank friends and colleagues who have read all or part of this book. Mark Atherton, Eoin de Bhaldraithe, O.Cist., Paul Bradshaw, Oliver Davies, Stuart Murray, Christopher Rowland, Mark Thiessen Nation, and Thomas Weinandy, O.F.M., Cap., have clarified my thinking and rescued me from many miscues; I am grateful to them, although I of course remain responsible for the indiscretions that remain. Eleanor Kreider has been my companion as we together have thought and taught about early Christianity; I am grateful for the insights that have grown as we have conversed, and for her careful reading of the text. I wish I had been able to share the book with John S. Oyer of Goshen College, Indiana, whose example inspired me to be a Christian and a historian. In thanksgiving, I dedicate this book to his memory.

# 1

# The Conversions of Justin And Cyprian

## Conversions in the New Testament

The four Gospels are full of conversion stories. Jesus would arrive in a town, fix his gaze on a tax collector or revolutionary, and say "Follow me." The persons addressed then had a choice—to submit to the comprehensive change that Jesus' invitation would bring to their lives or to "go away grieving" (Mark 10:22). Jesus' friendship was demanding; it led to upheavals in people's beliefs, in their sense of belonging, and in their behavior. As all four Gospel writers emphasize, Jesus buttressed his summons to discipleship with graphic teaching about its costs and rewards (e.g., John 15:12–20). Within a generation, these were being expressed by an initiation ritual, baptism, which, according to the missionary theologian Paul, dramatized the costs—conversion entailed the death of sinful patterns of living—and the rewards—there was rebirth to life under a new Lord as "slaves of righteousness" (Rom. 6:18). Conversion meant change.

When we turn to the narratives of the earliest church, as recorded in the Book of Acts, we find a puzzling mixture of patterns in the conversion stories. In some of these—the conversion of Paul being most notable—there are accounts (told in Paul's case no fewer than three times) of his transforming experience of the risen Christ, which shattered his

1

old assumptions and loyalties and reconfigured his life (Acts 9, etc.). Henceforth, the beliefs that sustained him and that he would debate *ad infinitum*, the solidarities that he would form with both Jews and Gentiles, and the behavior that he would manifest were radically transformed. With Peter, whose second conversion was also dramatic (and is told twice, Acts 10–11), there were also far-reaching changes in his belief, belonging, and behavior as he was tugged, against his better judgment, into a new world populated by Gentiles and enemies. For both Paul and Peter, conversion was costly. Henceforth their lives were risky and terminated by execution.

Other conversion stories, however, leave us wondering what changed. The centurion Cornelius, who shares the Acts 10 drama with Peter, experienced the filling of the Spirit and baptism. What happened to him? Did he leave the forces? Did his conversion change his lifestyle and priorities? The writer of Acts doesn't say. Or what happened to the Ethiopian eunuch who met the apostle Philip on the road (8:26ff)? At the eunuch's request, Philip baptized him and promptly disappeared, whereupon the eunuch "went on his way rejoicing" (8:39). He rejoiced, but did he change? These accounts leave us hanging in the air. Do they mean to convey that, in sectors of early Christianity, the change of conversion was not something that was assumed? By the fifth century this was clearly so, at least on the part of some North African laymen, to the consternation of Augustine of Hippo (Augustine, citing "our opponents," in *Faith and Works* 1.1; 6.9).

The opponents of Augustine were attempting to innovate. We can speculate what the centurion or eunuch did, but we cannot know. What we can report is that when, beginning in the second century, we get narratives of conversion, they indicate that change was—and had always been?—what conversion was all about. Let us begin by looking at Justin.

### The Stories of Justin's Conversion

Justin has left two accounts of his conversion.[1] The longer of these appears in his *Dialogue with Trypho*, a Jewish conversation partner. According to this account, Justin was a Gentile who came from Palestine; his birthplace was Flavia Neapolis near Samaria.[2] In about 130 C.E. Justin left home on a philosophical grand tour. As he traveled, he submitted himself to a succession of teachers—a Stoic, an Aristotelian, a Pythagorean, and a Platonist—from whom he sought knowledge of God. While he was in Ephesus and still a disciple of a "sagacious" Platonist, Justin went for a walk near the sea and encountered an ostensibly unremarkable old man, a Jewish Christian, with whom he began an extended conversation. The conversation changed his life. As he talked with the old man, "the gates of light" began to open. The Hebrew prophets, Justin learned, had foretold "events which have happened." And the most important of these was the coming of God's Son, the Christ, who had imparted a wisdom superior to all others. As Justin listened to the old man, he realized that "the words of the Savior" had a power that is both converting and pursuing: these words "possess a terrible power in themselves, and are sufficient to inspire those who turn aside from the path of rectitude with awe." These words also prescribed a way of living that is genuinely happy: "the sweetest rest is afforded to those who make a diligent practice of them." Christ's philosophy alone, Justin discovered, is "safe and profitable." For Justin, conversion involved a change of belief, and this new belief was to be sealed in an initiatory rite. At some point—Justin doesn't tell us when—he had a profound experience: "a flame was kindled in my soul."

Justin's shorter account, in his second *Apology* (12), is more personal and less philosophical. In it Justin tells how he, like many people, had heard rumors about the Christians' misbehavior—they were "living in wickedness and pleasure." But Justin then saw how the Christians functioned under pressure; when persecuted and tortured they were "fearless of death." Justin was impressed. The Christians' behavior made the rumors incredible; and as he explored their faith, his commitment to Platonism paled.

Two conversion accounts—is either credible, or are they literary fictions? Some scholars have concentrated on the contrasts (even contradictions) between the stories; others have attempted to harmonize them psychologically (Skarsaune 1976:53–55). A judicious reading by Henry Chadwick concludes that Justin's *Trypho* account, written after some years, was "an essentially veracious autobiography," although compressed and tailored to an apologetic context (1965:280); and Justin's second *Apology* account has many early Christian parallels.

### Catechizing for Comprehensive Change

But these accounts take Justin only to the threshold of faith; what was involved as people crossed the threshold to become Christians? We next meet Justin in Rome, to which he had migrated and where he had become a teacher. In rooms above the Timotinian baths he met with students who listened to him inculcate the beliefs and behavior of the Christians. He must have taught well. "I listened gladly to the teaching of Justin," one of his students commented (*Acts of Justin*, Recension B 2–3). Justin's varied past enabled him to relate his Christian convictions to other philosophical options. Justin also saw himself in the developing stream of Christian tradition: in his writings—especially his first *Apology*—the phrases "we have learned" and "we have been taught" are interspersed with his own teaching (1 *Apol* 10–13). So Justin functioned as a transmitter of the teaching of the churches in Rome; he may have provided catechetical instruction for baptismal candidates; and he enabled Roman Christians to advocate their faith to skeptical outsiders. From what Justin said about his own teaching, we may, I believe, infer something about conversion in the churches in Rome—and his own conversion.

In chapters 12–17 of his *Apology*, Justin summarized what he taught to his students. He taught about God's character— "temperance and righteousness and love of mankind"— which God showed in creation and in inspiring the prophets to foreshadow the coming of "our Teacher... who is the Son and Apostle of God the Father and Master of us all, that is, Jesus Christ, from whom we have received the name of Christians." Justin's teaching then turned from belief to behavior. His hearers, he knew, would have difficulty living out the teachings of Jesus; they would be locked in "struggle" with demons who would seek to deceive and enslave them with lures of "necessity"—which we may perhaps paraphrase as compulsion and addiction. If the inquirers were to overcome these, they must "struggle to their utmost for their own salvation." Christian leaders would "attack" the demons, possibly in exorcisms prior to baptism. But the Christian believers themselves, who have been "persuaded by the Word," were to renounce the demons and resist their thrall.[3]

Justin urged the Christians to resist the demons' power in three areas to which across the centuries pastoral theologians have been attuned—money, sex, and power—to which Justin added a fourth, the occult. These perennial areas of addiction and compulsion were clearly issues of conflict and conversion for Christians in Rome, and they may have been areas of struggle for Justin as well: repeatedly he used the word "we." The first area that he mentioned was sexual adventure: "we who once rejoiced in fornication now delight in continence alone." The second was occult practice: "we who made use of magic arts have dedicated ourselves to the good and unbegotten God." About the final two areas in which Christians had struggled for liberation, Justin wrote in even greater detail—acquisitive materialism: "we who once took most pleasure in the means of increasing our wealth and property now bring what we have into a common fund and share with everyone in need"; and xenophobic violence: "we who hated and killed one another and would not associate with men of different tribes because of [their different] customs, now after the manifestation of Christ live together and pray for our enemies."

For Justin, Christian *belief* led to a discerning of areas of demonic power in society that enslaved people; but the freedom that Christ brought liberated people from addiction and compulsion, and led to distinctive forms of *behavior*. It also led to a unique sense of *belonging*. The Christian community was knit together by its search for ways of dealing with sex, the occult, wealth, and violence that would be in keeping with the teachings of Jesus. A common fund, sharing with the needy, prayer for enemies—these built the corporate habits and institutions that are the essence of community. And these were only samples. In order to indicate the other possibilities of alternative behavior and belonging, Justin quoted at length from the teachings of Christ. These were difficult to live, but thanks to "the divine power" they were not impossible.

> We have learned that it is better to believe things impossible to our own nature... than to disbelieve like others, since we know that our Teacher Jesus Christ said, "The things that are impossible with men are possible with God" (1 *Apol* 14–17, 19).

### The Rites of Conversion in Justin's Rome

Justin does not tell us about his own baptism, but he indicated that for those seeking to espouse the Christian way baptism was the nodal point of conversion. Those approaching baptism submitted themselves to teaching. Correct belief was important—baptism was for those who "are persuaded and believe that the things we teach and say are true." So also was a reformation of behavior—baptism was for those who "promise that they can live" according to the teaching of the church (1 *Apol* 61). This was vital, for as Justin commented, "those who are found not living as [Christ] taught should know that they are not really Christians, even if his teachings are on their lips." Was this the time when the church's exorcists "attacked" the demons whose addictive wiles kept people in their thrall (1 *Apol* 14; 2 *Apol* 6)? We do not know. But Justin does tell us that in the prebaptismal period members of the Christian community (possibly including the catechists; Justin uses the word "we") joined the candidates in prayers and fasting. Justin says little about the baptismal rite itself or about the experience of the baptismal candidates. He simply reports that he and others brought the candidates to "where there is water," and there the candidates were reborn, washed, illuminated. Through baptism their sins were remitted, and they became God's children "of free choice and knowledge"—and thus brothers and sisters one of another. This entry into the new locus of belonging—the Christian church—was ritually articulated as the leaders and catechists (again Justin's "we") led the newly born believers "to those who are called brethren, where they are assembled." There, for the first time, they entered into the unitive activities of the family of faith—common prayer, the holy kiss, and the eucharistic meal (1 *Apol* 61, 65).

The sense of belonging with those who shared a common belief and way of living in Christ was palpable and durable. In 165 Justin was beheaded together with a group of people who had studied with him. Their diversity—Christians of both sexes, slave and free, of Cappadocian and Phrygian as well as Roman birth—shows how inclusive was the belonging into which the early Christians were converted (*Acts of Justin* 4, 6).

### Cyprian: Living in Gilded Torments

Our second early Christian conversion story is that of Cyprian, who became a Christian just before the middle of the third century in Carthage.[4] Cyprian was one of the province's high flyers, an aristocrat of outstanding rhetorical gift. But Cyprian found the lifestyle of his aristocratic class to be unsatisfying. He called it "darkness and gloomy night" (*Ad Donatum* 3).[5] Somehow, possibly through friendship with a venerable Christian presbyter called Caecilianus, Cyprian encountered the Christian community. The Christians, interpreted no doubt by Caecilianus, held out for Cyprian the possibility of a freedom that had eluded him.

But could he change? Cyprian surveyed his lifestyle. His behavior of costly consumption and his conspicuous exercise of power were characteristic of Roman aristocrats (MacMullen 1988:60–64). Cyprian ate only the best—he was "used to liberal banquets and sumptuous feasts." Cyprian wore exquisite clothing—he has "been glittering in gold and purple, and has been celebrated for his costly attire." Cyprian was surrounded by crowds of retainers—he "has felt the charm of the fasces [the symbol of authority of a superior magistrate] and... [is] dignified by the numerous association of an officious train" (*Ad Donatum* 3). Inspired perhaps by his encounter with Christians, Cyprian was deeply ambivalent about these aspects of his lifestyle. He was drawn to them, but he called them "gilded torments"; for him they had the appearance of "smiling wickedness." Cyprian sensed that these things, which offered the wealthy person the power of possession, in reality possessed their possessors. The rich person "is held in bondage by his gold, and... is the slave of his luxury and wealth rather than their master" (*Ad Donatum* 11–12). But Cyprian wanted to be free.

### Conversion: Empowerment to Do the Impossible

Was it possible? Cyprian, introduced by Caecilianus, was taken to the church where he became a catechumen. The sources do not tell what Cyprian studied during his catechumenate. They inform us that he sold lands and estates; also, that "as a catechumen he loved the poor" (Pontius, *Vita Cypriani* 6). Cyprian must have attempted to learn by observing the example of Christians, perhaps especially of Caecilianus, "the friend and comrade of his soul" (*Vita Cypriani* 4). But although his progress must have been rapid ("greater progress is made by faith than by time"), according to Cyprian things were anything but easy for him. From his own account we get a picture of profound inner turbulence. His struggle was not to believe what the Christians believed; rather, it was to live as they taught—and as many of them seem to have lived. Cyprian, encountering a community in which "thrift" and "ordinary and simple clothing" were normal, found that luxury was bred in his bones. "The errors of my previous life" were, he sensed, a part of his corrupted human nature; they were "actually parts of me... and indigenous to me." Furthermore, they were deeply etched on his person by long habit. "These things," he reported, "have become deeply and radically engrained within us." He was, to use our language, addicted to wealth and power. This filled him with despair, and he may have engaged in moments of frustrated recidivism ("I used to indulge my sins")(*Ad Donatum* 3–4).

But as a catechumen on the road to membership in the Christian church, Cyprian was among people who were learning to live differently. The task was too great for him; the spiritual challenge of conversion was daunting. Cyprian, unlike Justin, did not use the vocabulary of demonic oppression to describe his struggle. Exorcisms were no doubt a part of his initiatory program, but his discussion of exorcism in *Ad Donatum* was probably not directly related to his own struggles (*Ad Donatum* 5; *Ep* 75[69].15). In contrast, Cyprian presented baptism as the decisive turning point. Caecilianus, as "the parent of his new life," evidently accompanied Cyprian as he approached baptism. Into Cyprian's sense that change was impossible flowed the "water of new birth" and "the agency of the Spirit breathed from heaven." In the Carthage church's rituals of immersion and anointing Cyprian had a powerful experience of washing and empowerment. "In a wondrous manner," he reported, "what before had seemed difficult began to suggest a means of accomplishment; what had been thought impossible, to be capable of being achieved." It was through baptism that Cyprian became not only a Christian; he became a free man, an ex-addict endowed with "liberty and power" (*Ad Donatum* 4–5).

Shortly after his baptism, Cyprian was vaulted into leadership in the Christian community in Carthage. It was a time of recurrent persecution as well as of a mass epidemic, both of which were supreme challenges to his leadership. As a bishop he is reported to have lived simply and hospitably, with his home open to the poor. His clothing, which had been so important to him before his conversion, was "subdued to a fitting mean" (*Vita Cypriani* 3, 6). When in 258 he came to be executed, he was wearing an outer cloak and a dalmatic—but no purple (*Acta Cypriani* 5)! For he had been converted, and his behavior, like his beliefs and his sense of belonging, had been conformed to those of the Christian community.

# 2

# The Intriguing Attraction of Early Christianity

## Growing Despite Disincentives

Justin and Cyprian were both converts; they also were martyrs.[1] They were executed for their membership in a movement that was marginal, liminal, on the fringes of polite and respectable society. Like all early Christians, they had to contend with a popular epithet for members of dissident groups—"insane." And they knew that popular hostility or governmental initiative could lead to persecution, deportation, or death. Yet they, and an ever-increasing number of people, persisted in converting to Christianity. Statistics are of course nonexistent, and all estimates are highly approximate, which must allow for wide regional variation throughout the Roman Empire. However, a recent study by Rodney Stark has made a fascinating observation. If, as many scholars now agree, at the time of the emperor Constantine's legalization of Christianity in 312, approximately 10 percent of the imperial population belonged to the Christian church, then during the previous three centuries the churches statistically grew at an average of 40 percent per decade (Stark 1996:8). That is impressive. Despite disincentives, despite the scorn of the powerful, despite persecutions, the early Christian movement was growing. Something was deeply attractive about it.

To determine what attracted people, it is worth listening to contemporaries, both hostile and committed, who shed important light while addressing other questions. A hostile witness is the Carthaginian pagan Caecilius, who at around the turn of the third century made these observations:

> [The Christians are] a gang... of discredited and proscribed desperadoes who band themselves against the gods. Fellows who gather together illiterates from the dregs of the populace and credulous women with the instability natural to their sex, and so organize a rabble of profane conspirators, leagued together by meetings at night and ritual fasts and unnatural repasts... a secret tribe that shuns the light, silent in the open, but talkative in hid corners.... Root and branch it must be exterminated and accursed. They [the Christians] recognize one another by secret signs and marks; they fall in love almost before they are acquainted; everywhere they introduce a kind of religion of lust, a promiscuous "brotherhood" and "sisterhood" by which ordinary fornication, under the cover of a hallowed name, is converted to incest (Minucius Felix, *Octavius* 8.4;9.1–2).

Caecilius noted that the Christians were members of a "secret" and "silent" movement; they were—of necessity, the early Christians might have retorted—not a public force. Caecilius was outraged by the movement: it conspired to oppose the accepted public religion, which secured the public welfare, and its ways of worship and life violated conventional values. And yet Caecilius was also fascinated by the movement; he and others were quite content to pass on rumors about what Christians did behind closed doors. As he said later of the Christian worship services, "Their form of feasting is notorious; it is in everyone's mouth" (*Octavius* 9.6). So the Christians, although offensive, were intriguing; they were rumor-worthy. And what especially interested Caecilius was the Christians' behavior and their sense of

belonging. They gathered at night, bringing together for their
ritual meals a socially scandalous inclusivity of the populace.
Religious clubs ought to be exclusive, but the Christians
brought together women (unstable and credulous) along with
no doubt stable and incredulous men, illiterate people along
with literates. What could they possibly have in common?
Their bonding was surprising, knitting together people by
love and rite into a brotherhood/sisterhood of promiscuous
belonging. Caecilius wasn't interested in joining this movement; but he took it seriously, and he paid it the compli-
ments of gossip and attack.

## Question-Posing Behavior

Let us compare this passage with the comments of a
Christian writing in North Africa at approximately the same
time—Tertullian. Tertullian's concern in his essay *To His
Wife* was to argue against second marriages by Christian widows, especially against marriages to pagans. In describing the
problems that such a "mixed" marriage would cause for the
believing woman, Tertullian gives an intriguing picture of the
life of the Christian community in Carthage.

> For who would suffer his wife, for the sake of visiting
> the brethren, to go round from street to street to other
> men's, and indeed to all the poorer, cottages? Who will
> willingly bear her being taken from his side by noc-
> turnal convocations, if need so be? Who, finally, will
> without anxiety endure her absence all the night long
> at the paschal solemnities? Who will, without some
> suspicion of his own, dismiss her to attend the Lord's
> Supper which they defame? Who will suffer her to
> creep into prison to kiss a martyr's bonds? nay, truly,
> to meet any of the brethren to exchange the kiss? to
> offer water for the saints' feet? to snatch (somewhat
> for them) from her food, from her cup? to yearn (after
> them)? to have (them) in her mind? If a pilgrim broth-
> er arrive, what hospitality for him in an alien home?...
> [Such a wife is] a terror to her Gentile husband.... He

has felt "mighty works (*magnalia*)"; he knows her changed for the better: thus even he himself is, by his fear, a candidate for God (*To His Wife* 2.4, 7).

Like Caecilius, Tertullian presented a movement that met secretly, nocturnally, and in ways that aroused suspicion and concern. What do the Christians do at the Lord's Supper? What keeps them up all night at Easter? Who wants his wife to be gone all night anyway? Whatever the movement's meetings were like, they resulted in forms of belonging and behavior that were extraordinary. Why should a well-off pagan woman join a voluntary community about whose members' welfare she is passionately interested? Why should she go into the hovels of the poor? Why should she enter prison to visit the martyrs or kiss their chains—or (worse) kiss one of the brethren? Why should she invite a visiting "brother" to stay in their home? Or share her food and drink with other church members? All these things were disturbing for the non-Christian husband, and question posing. Becoming a Christian has changed his wife—"for the better," says Tertullian. The husband has also encountered a community in which supernatural power resides; in it the "mighty works" are a part of life. The husband, in coping with his wife, has a choice. He can attempt to obstruct his wife's Christian activities—for example, by ordering his wife to meet him at the baths at the moment when he knows the church has a meeting (2.5); or he can decide to investigate Christianity for himself. Men, like women, according to Tertullian, became Christians because the Christians, marginal though they were, were intriguingly attractive.

This attractiveness was the key to the churches' growth. Caecilius's fascination expresses this implicitly; Tertullian states it explicitly. But the churches were not growing for other reasons that we might expect. Neither Caecilius nor Tertullian referred to public witness, for this did not exist. The early Christians were "silent in the open." At least from the 60s C.E. they were members of a proscribed *superstitio*; if they advocated their faith in the forum, they could get not only themselves but their congregations into deathly difficulty.

The closest the early Christians came to making public statements came on the relatively rare occasions when, in the amphitheaters, they suffered exemplary execution. But even there their wordless behavior could elicit questions. Why do the Christians—male and female, well-born and common, slave and free—in extremis, just before being killed, exchange the kiss of peace (*Passio Perpetuae* 21)? How different they were from the rest of the populace, among whom "equals kissed on the level" (MacMullen 1988:63)! Nor did the Christians have explicit programs of evangelization. They thought and taught extensively about how believers should live and how their churches' common life should be ordered, but they had no "decades of evangelism" (Kreider 1995:6–7).

## Worship that Shapes an Attractive People

Nor did churches grow because their worship was attractive. From the second century onward, nonbelievers were barred from the Christian assemblies. In a world in which Christianity was illicit, the churches, fearing the arrival of spies and informers, assigned deacons to stand at the door to screen those attempting to come in. Were the people seeking entry "lambs or wolves" (*Testamentum Domini* 1.36)? Only the former were allowed in. And of these, only those who had been baptized were allowed to attend both the service of the word and the eucharistic service that followed; the others, admitted as catechumens but not yet baptized, were allowed only to attend the readings and teaching before being dismissed. Christian worship was designed to enable Christians to worship God. It was not designed to attract non-Christians; it was not "seeker-sensitive," for seekers were not allowed in.

If Christian worship did assist in the outreach of the churches, it did so incidentally, as a by-product, by shaping the consciousness of the individual Christians and the character of their communities so that their lives—and their interactions with outsiders—would be attractive and question posing. A sample of this comes from mid–third-century Syria. According to an anonymous church order—the *Didascalia*

*Apostolorum* (2.58)—the bishop was to be sure that a visiting poor man or woman should have a place to sit, "especially if they are stricken in years." If there was no place for them to sit, the document directed: "Do thou, O bishop, with all thy heart provide a place for them, even if thou have to sit upon the ground; that thou be not as one who respects the persons of men." With such an example from the community's president, other members might be reminded that they also were to "minister diligently [to the poor] and refresh them" (4.10). Christian worship thus assisted in the outreach of the churches indirectly, as a by-product, by shaping the lives and character of individual Christians and their communities so that they would be intriguingly vital (Kreider 1995:10).

## Inculturating the Faith

What then was it that was attractive about the early Christians? In the unsettled world of late antiquity, the Christians seemed to advocate and incarnate approaches to living that were both novel and comprehensible. They brought news that was new, that brought new perspectives and possibilities. But they expressed these in a symbolic and social language that was familiar and that addressed people's questions and struggles. Comprehensibility and critique— both were implicitly present in the Christians' self-identity as "resident aliens" (*paroikoi*). This was a familiar legal term, which many Christians from 1 Peter throughout the early centuries used to express their sense of identification with cultures in which they nevertheless embodied new approaches and insights (Labriolle 1927). The Christians, as one of their most eloquent early documents put it,

> live in their own countries, but only as resident aliens.
> They have a share in everything as citizens, and
> endure everything as foreigners. Every foreign land is
> their fatherland, and yet for them every fatherland is
> a foreign land (*Ep to Diognetus* 5.5).

Had the Christians not thus "inculturated" their message, had they not built on existing social patterns and borrowed

from the repertoire of myth and visual image of their sur-
roundings, their movement would have died. It is fascinating to
watch them as they adopted visual motifs in classical culture—
the shepherd Orpheus as the good shepherd, the praying figure
(*orante*), the dove, and the boat. Sometimes they succeeded
in giving these new meaning; sometimes the images' prior
meaning may have shaped what the ordinary Christians
believed (Wessels 1994:34–36). Often the early Christians
seem to have expressed themselves well—verbally, socially,
ritually, and visually—to communicate to their cultures and
to critique them, expressing insights and approaches that
were attractive in their plausibility and relevance.

## Beliefs and Power

For some, such as Justin, it was the beliefs of the Christians
that were the initial attraction. A few of the early stories of
conversion emphasize the intellectual element; and the work
of the apologists—such as Aristeides, Athenagoras, and Justin
himself—assisted in the expansion of the new faith by providing necessary confirmation of its theoretical resilience (Lane
Fox 1986:334). Without doubt, an important element in early
Christianity's success was the Christian belief that because
Christ had conquered death Christians need not fear death,
for they, on the last day, will rise to be with him. Movements
animated by this belief can withstand persecution (Cyprian,
*De Mortalitate; Ad Quirinum* 3.58). The documents at our
disposal—especially those produced by intellectuals—provide
some evidence that people were attracted by the Christians'
beliefs. But they also provide indication that people were
attracted to Christianity by two other realities, both of which
we have already encountered in the accounts of Caecilius
and Tertullian.

One of these was the sense that there was divine power
among the Christians. As Tertullian put it, the Christians
were in "touch with the miraculous." People possessing gifts
of healing were an accepted part of many Christian communities; their gifting was indicated "by a revelation" and by
"the facts"—did people get better (*Apostolic Tradition* 14)?

Even more important was the role of exorcism. Many ancient writers pointed to the role of exorcism in conversion; indeed, Ramsay MacMullen has claimed that this was "the chief instrument of conversion" (1984:27). This seems somewhat overstated. But we have already observed how, to Justin, the world was contested terrain in which demons, despite Christ's work on the cross, persisted in asserting their addictive authority. Many people felt themselves to be oppressed by predatory spiritual forces from which they longed for liberation. As a result, liberation from demonic power was one of the chief benefits that the churches could offer to potential converts (Ferguson 1984:129). It is not accidental that exorcisms became a central part of the initiatory rites of most Christian communities. The Christian communities could also experience the presence of demonic powers in more unpredictable ways. A sample of this comes from Palestine, where Origen—the early church's preeminent theologian— in the 240s was instructing catechumens from the Book of 1 Samuel. Suddenly, when he uttered the words of Hannah's prayer ("My heart has exulted in the Lord"), someone attending "was filled with an impure spirit" and cried out. Other attendees rushed to the stricken person, while Origen continued to declaim Hannah's words. Eventually the sufferer was set free. Origen then commented: "Things like this lead many people to be converted to God, many to reform themselves, many to come to faith" (*Hom on Sam* 1.10). In Gaul, a thousand miles to the West, Irenaeus observed similar things: people who have been delivered by acts of miraculous power "frequently both believe and join themselves to the church" (Adv Haer 2.32.4).[2] Believing and belonging could thus come about through experience in which people apprehended the superior power of the Christian God.

## Beauty of Life

The second reality was the Christians' behavior; as Tertullian put it, conversion changed the convert "into a better person" (*To His Wife* 2.7). Christian apologists made much of this. For example, Octavius, in his response to Caecilius, claimed

that "beauty of life encourages... strangers to join the ranks....
We do not preach great things, but we live them" (*Octavius*
31.7; 38.6). This was rather bold, and there must have been
innumerable early Christians whose behavior belied their
pretensions. An indication of this comes from a second-
century sermon:

> When the heathen hear God's oracles on our lips they
> marvel at their beauty and greatness. But afterwards,
> when they mark that our deeds are unworthy of the
> words we utter, they turn from this to scoffing, and say
> that it is a myth and a delusion. When for instance,
> they hear from us that God says, "It is no credit to you
> if you love those who love you, but it is to your credit
> if you love your enemies and those who hate you,"
> when they hear these things, they are amazed at such
> surpassing goodness. But when they see that we fail to
> love not only those who hate us, but even those who
> love us, then they mock at us and scoff at the Name (2
> Clement 13.4).

But note that the preacher was reminding his flock that it
was their task to embody attractive new possibilities; their
failure should not keep them from trying again. And this possibility of transformed behavior seems to have been a message that even lower-class Christians communicated. Late in
the second century, the pagan critic Celsus reported that
"the most illiterate and bucolic yokels" claimed that "they
alone... know the right way to live" (Origen, *Contra Celsum*
3.55). How exasperating! But this self-confidence, alarming
to a pagan, indicated that Christians sensed that their way of
life was deeply attractive.

How was this lifestyle shaped? In part, as we will note in
Chapter 3, the behavior of the Christians was the product of
careful prebaptismal catechizing by church leaders who
attempted to apply the teachings of Christ to the lives of their
flock. Furthermore, the Christians' lifestyle was the product
of their self-identity: as "resident aliens" they were members
of a church whose social reality spanned and transcended the

Roman Empire. "To the Christian, the whole of this world is our home" (Pontius, *Vita Cypriani* 11). Christian congregations expressed this reality by corresponding with other churches, by providing hospitality to travelers (early Christians were an exceptionally mobile lot [Wischmeyer 1992:61]), and by supporting fellow Christians who were prisoners doing service in the mines (Aristeides, *Apol* 15.8). And yet, locally, they also knew that they were a body of people with a big vision living an unusual lifestyle. "The Christian is a stranger even in his own city" (Pontius, *Vita Cypriani* 11). In some communities this was evidenced by empowering of the weak, including giving an unusual freedom to women to do significant things, as Tertullian (who was by no means a feminist) nevertheless indicated (MacDonald 1996). Even more broadly, the early Christian communities were marked by economic sharing and a solicitous care for the poor—and not only their own poor!

A fascinating example comes from early fourth-century Egypt, where press gangs were abducting peasants and shipping them down the Nile for service in the Roman legions. In Thebes the Christian church heard of conscripts in their local jail; the military authorities had put them there to prevent them from escaping before they transported them further. When the Christians heard that the prisoners were in distress, they brought them food, drink, and other necessities. One of the conscripts, Pachomius, asked what was going on. The people coming to his aid, he was told, were Christians who "are merciful to everyone, including strangers." Pachomius had never heard of Christians, so he asked for more information.

> They are people who bear the name of Christ, the only begotten Son of God, and they do good to everyone, putting their hope in Him who made the heaven and earth and us humans (*First Greek Life of Pachomius* 4–5).

Inspired by the Christians' visit and material aid, Pachomius sought as much solitude as was possible in the

# 3

# The Journey of Conversion

### The Four Stages of Resocialization

A community of compassion—this is the kind of church that attracted Pachomius. For him and for other inquirers into the faith, conversion involved becoming the kind of person who belonged to that kind of community. This could not happen quickly. It could come about only when candidates submitted themselves to a process of "resocialization" by which their new community superintended the transformation of their beliefs, their sense of belonging, and their patterns of behavior (Meeks 1993:12). No longer would they live by the values of the dominant society. A process of examination, instruction, and ritual rehabituated the candidates for conversion, re-reflexing them into the lifestyle of an alternative community.[1]

How this happened must have varied from one Christian community to another. But from documents in North Africa and Palestine, as well as the celebrated and enigmatic *Apostolic Tradition*, which has conventionally been attributed to Hippolytus, we learn of a journey of conversion. In its fully developed fourth-century form, according to the analysis of contemporary liturgists, it commonly had four stages (Harmless 1995:3). In Stage 1, evangelization, contact between Christians and a potential believer was informal and depended on the particular experience of each person. It ended when those who were attracted to Christianity approached the church leaders and applied for instruction. If the leaders, having examined the candidates, gave them their approval, the leaders admitted the candidate to Stage 2—the catechumenate. Now the candidates, having left behind their old values and solidarities, were committed to the journey of conversion. As catechumens, the candidates were no longer conventional pagans, nor were they yet members of the Christian community. Several times a week they received instruction conducive to the conversion process. The teaching seems to have concentrated on a reshaping of the converts' *behavior*. When a candidate's behavior was adjudged to have changed sufficiently, he or she was admitted to Stage 3—enlightenment—which concentrated upon *belief*. In this stage the catechists were concerned to impart to their candidates orthodox teaching; the candidates also received exorcisms and other spiritual preparations culminating in the baptismal rites through which the catechumens were "born in water" (Tertullian, *On Baptism* 1). At this point they experienced *belonging*, as full members of the Christian community; they could take part in the community's prayers and eucharist. In the fourth century, a brief Stage 4 was added—mystagogy—in which the catechists in the week after Easter explained the meaning of the rites (baptism and eucharist) and *experience* in which the new believers had just participated.

## Conversion in the *Apostolic Tradition*

The earliest source that provides detail on this process is the *Apostolic Tradition*, which apparently records the practice of various third-century churches.[2] According to the *Apostolic Tradition* (15–16), a person who through the friendships characteristic of the informal Stage 1 had decided to join a Christian community approached a friend or sponsor, who on a weekday morning accompanied him or her to meet with Christian teachers before one of the church's regular catechetical sessions. In this first encounter or "scrutiny," which was the link to Stage 2, the teachers did not welcome the potential candidates with open arms. Instead, they asked hard questions, both of the sponsors and of the potential candidates, about the candidates' status, jobs, and behavior. The catechists' concern was to determine whether the candidates were "capable of hearing the word." Were they living in a way that would enable them to understand the church's teachings? What was the marital state of the candidates? If the candidates were slaves, what did their masters think? Were the candidates involved in some profession that involved behavior that the church repudiated— idolatry, astrology, killing, or sexual looseness? If so, "Let them cease or be rejected." If a person was in a difficult profession, such as military service, they could be accepted into the ranks of the catechumens only if they promised not to kill. If a soldier took life or if a catechumen joined the legions, "Let him be rejected." This may seem severe and legalistic to us today, even perverse. How could a community rebuff people as potential members for not living according to the standards of the group *before* they had been taught? But the early Christian catechists were attempting not so much to impart concepts as to nurture communities whose values would be different from those of conventional society. Christian leaders assumed that people did not think their way into a new life; they lived their way into a new kind of thinking (Rohr 1991:59). The candidates' socialization and their professions and life commitments would determine whether they could receive what the Christian community considered to be good news.

Having passed the first scrutiny and been accepted for teaching, the catechumens had embarked on Stage 2 of their conversion journey. Early in the morning several times a week, the candidates, at times accompanied by their sponsors, met to "hear the word." When the instructor had finished teaching, the catechumens and the believers divided into separate groups. While the believers prayed and exchanged "the peace," the catechumens prayed by themselves without giving the peace ("for their kiss is not yet holy"). Then, when the teacher had laid hands on them and prayed for them, he dismissed them and they went to work. This regimen of daily catechesis could last what seems to us a remarkable length of time. The Sahidic (Coptic) recension of the *Apostolic Tradition* (of the late third century?) says it could last for three years; and in early fourth-century Spain, the catechumenate could last for five years (Hamman 1992:151; *Canons of Elvira* 11). But the aim was not duration but conversion, so the catechumenate could be much shorter than that: "if a man is keen, and perseveres well in the matter, the time shall not be judged, but only his conduct" (*Ap Trad* 17).

The *Apostolic Tradition* says disappointingly little about the content of catechism. It makes clear that the example of church members, including the sponsors, was very important in guiding the behavior of the catechumens. As members encouraged the behavior of catechumens, the teachings of Jesus must have been formative, for "you have Christ always in memory" (*Ap Trad* 41). The concerns of the scrutiny—the examination at the climax of their catechumenate—had to do with practical matters; this must also say a lot about what the catechists were trying to teach the catechumens. By example and instruction, the catechists were intentionally re-forming the candidates' conduct. And the extent to which this re-formation was successful would determine whether the candidates could proceed further in their journey of conversion. If the candidates and their sponsors agreed that they were living like Christians, they appeared together before the community's leaders, who performed a second scrutiny, this time of the candidates' conduct and lifestyle:

> Have they lived good lives when they were catechumens? Have they honored the widows? Have they visited the sick? Have they done every kind of good work? (*Ap Trad* 20).

If the sponsors could report that the candidates had indeed been living according to the values and priorities of the Christian community, then they could enter Stage 3 of their journey. As the *Apostolic Tradition* (20) enjoins: "Let them hear the gospel."

From this time forward, in the final weeks prior to their baptism, the candidates attended catechism daily. The *Apostolic Tradition* does not specify what the "gospel" meant, and this has caused scholars some puzzlement. It seems possible that this was shorthand for the process by which the catechists introduced the catechumens to the beliefs of the church in the form of nascent creeds—the local "rules of faith"—and warned them of the dangers of various heresies; during this time the catechumens may also for the first time have encountered the Lord's Prayer.[3] They also received a daily exorcism. As the time of their baptism approached, the bishop performed a third and final scrutiny of each candidate. This time the scrutiny was an exorcism. The bishop's concern was whether the candidates were "pure," able to "hear the word with faith" because the "Alien" had been completely banished.

If so, the candidates approached the climax of Stage 3 of their journey of conversion—the cathartic rituals of the Easter vigil. On Saturday the bishop summoned the candidates and exorcised them a final time and breathed into their faces. Then the candidates were disrobed and anointed. Naked, their "secular socialization" was dismantled, and they left behind their "lifelong accumulation of secular interests, values and loyalties" (Miles 1989:24). They renounced Satan and were immersed three times, confessing their faith in the Father, the Son and the Holy Spirit. As they ascended from the water they were clad anew. Then, at long last, they "entered into the church." The bishop anointed them and signed them with the cross, whereupon the candidates were incorporated as brothers and sisters into a new family. This belonging afforded them solidarity: among the church's members they would find brothers and sisters in a new family—and their new primary locus of belonging. It also offered them danger: until 312 Christianity was an illicit superstition, and "every Christian was a candidate for death" (Bardy 1949:170).

The new believers' entry was not quite complete. For the first time, they participated in the family's activities of common prayer and "the kiss of peace" and received the nourishing bread, wine, milk, and honey of their first eucharist. Their beliefs, belonging, and behavior had been transformed through their journey of conversion, and the catechumens were now "Christians," newly born (neophytes) to be sure, but fully members of the Christian church. As such, the new Christians might receive some private instruction by the bishop about the sacraments that they had now experienced. But for them the main task was to live as Christians; they were to "hasten to do good works... and to conduct themselves rightly, being zealous for the Church, doing what they have learned" (*Ap Trad* 21).[4]

### The Catechumens' Learning—
### Narratives and Controlling Images

But what, we might well ask, had the catechumens learned? Scholars have given little attention to this; but because conversion involved change, and change was a prerequisite for baptism, it is important for us to try to do a bit of detective work. From other sources, which are a bit more communicative than the *Apostolic Tradition*, we can get a few hints about what had been taught during Stage 2 of the journey. There seem to have been at least four categories of material that were taught to those undergoing conversion.

One of these—which may have been central to the catechists' teachings—was the fund of narratives of the Christian communities. The earliest believers, Cyprian's biographer Pontius noted, had not required a lengthy catechism or prebaptismal preparation. Candidates such as the Ethiopian eunuch (Acts 8) already knew the Hebrew Scriptures, with its teachings and narratives. But candidates who came from "the ignorant pagans"—even one as highly motivated as Cyprian—needed to be taught the narratives of the tradition that he was exploring (Pontius, *Vita Cypriani* 3). So it is not surprising that in Irenaeus' *Proof of the Apostolic Preaching* there is a narrative structure to the catechesis (Ferguson

1989). In a far more expansive and leisurely form, this was also true of Origen's catechetical homilies on the books of the Hebrew Scriptures. And, two centuries later, Augustine was deeply concerned that his baptismal candidates be shaped by the church's fund of narratives (Harmless 1995:149). It was important that Christians had a sense of the sweep of history as well as life-giving role models.

The catechists were concerned, in the second place, to impart what we might call controlling images—pictures or stories that gave a sense of identity to the Christian community. Some of these, such as the three young men in the fiery furnace of Daniel 3 or the miracles of Christ the healer, recur frequently in frescoes in the catacombs; they expressed realities that the Christians had experienced (Snyder 1985:54–55, 59). Another example is the prophetic passage that early Christian writers cited more often than any other—Isaiah 2:2–4/Micah 4:1–4 (Lohfink 1986). This passage, which Origen assumed all Christians knew, must have been imparted in catechism:

> For who of all believers does not know the words in Isaiah? "And in the last days the mountain of the Lord shall be manifest, and the house of the Lord on the top of the mountains, and it shall be exalted above the hills; and all nations shall come unto it. And many people shall go and say, 'Come ye, and let us go up to the mountain of the Lord, unto the house of the God of Jacob; and He will teach us his way, and we will walk in it.' For out of Zion shall go forth a law, and a word of the Lord from Jerusalem. And he shall judge among the nations, and shall rebuke many people; and they shall beat their swords into ploughshares, and their spears into pruning-hooks. Nation shall not lift up sword against nation, neither shall they learn war any more" (*Ep to Julius Africanus* 15).

Not surprisingly, early Christian writers cited this passage's controlling image repeatedly in a wide variety of literature.[5]

### The Catechumens' Learning—
### How to Put Jesus' Teachings into Practice

A third category of material may, for some early Christian teachers, have been an example of the "new law" that went forth from Jerusalem—the teaching of Jesus Christ. The second-century apologist Aristeides observed, "Now the Christians... have the commandments of the Lord Jesus Christ himself engraven on their hearts, and these they observe" (*Apol* 15.3). Later in the century the Athenian Athenagoras, when asked "what... are the teachings on which we are brought up?" responded by quoting Jesus' Sermon on the Mount: "I say to you, love them who curse you, pray for them who persecute you, that you may be sons of your Father in heaven" (*Legatio* 11.2). According to Origen, it was Jesus who takes charge of the believer and "becomes the guide of their new journey" (*Hom on Joshua* 4.2). His sayings, Justin commented, "were short and concise... [and] his word was the power of God" (1 *Apol* 14). So Christians learned—and were no doubt taught by their catechists—the "precepts" and "maxims" of the Lord whose words were "powerful," "incisive," and full of "charm."[6] His life also became a model. Believers, faced with hostility, were to "follow Jesus as a pattern of the way to endure religious persecution" (Origen, *Contra Celsum* 2.25). Catechumens were to "imitate his teaching and his behavior" (*Didascalia Apostolorum* 5.5). Thus taught, they would be ready to become members of communities whose members "undertake the life which Jesus taught, the life which leads everyone who lives according to Jesus' commandments to friendship with God and fellowship with Jesus" (Origen, *Contra Celsum* 3.28).

Finally, the catechists imparted practical teaching. Their success as teachers would be measured by the extent to which their students learned the ways of the Christian community, and learned these so well that they became habituative. What did they teach? In some communities, no doubt—if we can generalize upon the *Apostolic Tradition's* primary criterion—the catechists were concerned to be alert to the needs of poor people. Another source hints that the catechumens were taught how to confess their faith when under interrogation and how, when persecuted, to be steadfast (*Didascalia Apostolorum* 5.6). Origen reported that the catechumens were taught not to defend themselves against their enemies, but to respond with "gentleness and love to man" (*Contra Celsum* 3.8). As Origen emphasized, central to the task of the catechist was "changing the conduct and habits" of the catechumens so that they would "show the fruits worthy of conversion" (*Hom on Luke* 22.5, 8). And in this, according to one of Origen's star pupils, Gregory of Pontus, it was the example of the catechists themselves that was truly life changing. Origen, he reported, "incited us much more to the practice of virtue, and stimulated us by the deeds he did more than by the doctrines he taught" (*Panegyric* 9).

### The "Religious Teaching" of Cyprian's School

A source that may be especially helpful to us is Cyprian's *Ad Quirinum*, which may indicate what Cyprian thought ought to be on the agenda for catechists and catechumens. In response to a request from a certain Quirinus, who may have been a catechist, Cyprian compiled three books of precepts, each precept buttressed by a string of biblical quotations (Quacquarelli 1971:204). The first book deals with salvation history (especially the Christian church's relationship to Judaism), the second with Christology. The third book, which is more than twice as long as the other two put together, is more comprehensive, providing "certain precepts of the Lord, and divine teachings" that relate to "the religious teaching of our school." Cyprian hoped this would be "easy and useful" (*Ad Quirinum* preface). The 120 precepts had two functions. Primarily, they dealt with qualities that characterized the Christian churches as communities of distinctive belief, belonging, and behavior. Furthermore, because Cyprian buttressed each of these 120 precepts with a brace of biblical texts, they served to increase the biblical knowledge of the communities.

Forty-eight of Book III's 120 precepts emphasized belief. Precept 10: "We must trust in God only, and in him we must

glory." Another precept assured the believers that they were
secure, in a world ominous with plague and persecution, for
God provides resurrection. Therefore "no one should be
made sad by death"—and, by implication, every Christian
could take risks of obedience (3.58). For Cyprian, the
eucharist was central to the community's worship; it was "to
be received with fear and honor." But what really mattered
to Cyprian about the community's beliefs and sacraments
was how they affected the community's practice: "It is of
small account to be baptized and to receive the eucharist,"
according to precept 26, "unless one profit by it both in
deeds and works." What the community believed mattered,
not least because it affected how the community behaved.

If belief was important to Cyprian, so also was belonging.
Cyprian in many precepts sought to catechize a community
that would have a strong sense of shared identity. He used
familial language and emphasized that the family was to be
interdependent: "Brethren ought to support one another"
(3.9). Cyprian assumed that the supportive, interdependent
community would be socially distinctive: in several precepts
he emphasized that "the believer ought not to live like the
Gentile" (3.34, 62). Nor, when they had disputes, were they
to take their cases before "a Gentile judge" (3.44).

The greatest proportion of Cyprian's precepts had to do
with behavior. Cyprian wanted the believers to relate cre-
atively to non-Christians. Christians were to pay just wages
and not take usury (3.81, 48). When they were wounded
they were not to retaliate (3.23). Intriguingly, nowhere in the
120 precepts did Cyprian urge the Christians to speak to
non-Christians about their faith. Did he think this was too
dangerous? Or that the Christians' distinctive lifestyle would
be more eloquent than words? The latter seems likely: in
precept 26 he quotes passages having to do with an exemplary, visible lifestyle: "Let your light so shine before men."
And in precept 96 his concern was "that we must labor not
with words, but with deeds."

In light of this, it is not surprising that the bulk of the precepts of *Ad Quirinum* have to do with how Christians should

treat each other. So Cyprian dealt with good speech, anger, the importance of mutual correction, and good relationships within households. Cyprian, we are not surprised to note, had a high view of leadership: "We must rise when a bishop or a presbyter comes" (3.85). But he cautioned "that those are more severely judged, who in this world have had more power" (3.112). Cyprian wanted the believers to experience, within the framework of a viable and sustainable community, a life free of the forms of bondage he had known. In view of his own struggles in conversion, it is understandable that Cyprian dealt with simplicity of food, the dangers of acquisitiveness, and the lures of ostentatious living (3.60, 61, 36). Is the order of the 120 precepts significant, we might wonder? Not in general, I believe; but it cannot be accidental that his first precept has to do with "good works and mercy" that expressed themselves in economic redistribution. This had been a conversion issue for Cyprian, and the precept's thirty-six supportive biblical texts showed the depth of his own study and engagement. The first biblical passage cited in *Ad Quirinum* 3 was Isaiah 58:7: "Break thy bread to the hungry, and bring the homeless poor into thy house. If thou seest the naked, clothe him" (3.1). This is in keeping with the *Apostolic Tradition* in which attentiveness to the poor and needy was the primary area in which catechumens must manifest change if they were to proceed to baptism.

*Ad Quirinum* 3 may thus indicate what Cyprian thought catechists should teach in Stage 2 of the journey of conversion. Stage 3, of course, would require teaching in the more dogmatic areas of the Christian faith. Would *Ad Quirinum* 2 have provided material for this? In any event, baptism, at the culmination of Stage 3, provided the decisive threshold beyond which was the "enclosed garden" of the Christian community (Cyprian, *Ep* 73 [74].11). As a result of the changes that had taken place in each individual's journey of conversion, this garden would contain a network of relationships and a quality of life that would be distinctive. Its members would flourish and grow in freedom. Cyprian knew that this freedom had eluded him as a pagan, but he now believed

# 4

# Constantine Broadens the Attraction

## Delaying the Emperor's Conversion

In the course of the fourth century, Christians came to see the world from another vantage point. At the century's outset, the Christian church was undergoing a systematic, empirewide persecution. The incidence of the persecution varied; it was most severe in the East, but all Christian communities would have been aware of the danger—immediate or potential—in which they stood. In October 312 this danger ended when the Emperor-claimant Constantine defeated his rival Maxentius in battle on the edges of Rome. Constantine, on the eve of the battle, reported a vision in which he received an order to paint "the heavenly sign" of the cross on his soldiers' shields.[1] The following day his troops were victorious, and the capital—and with it the western Roman Empire—lay open to Constantine's control. In gratitude, Constantine sent for Christian priests, inquiring "who that God was, and what was intended by the sign of the vision" that he had seen (Eusebius, *Vita Constantini* [*VC*] 1.32). Constantine's response to their instruction was positive; so he admitted the priests to his entourage and proceeded—in the Edict of Milan of 313—to legalize Christianity, restoring its properties that the imperial authorities had confiscated, and giving it a position of privileged equality with other religions.[2]

Had Constantine thereby become a Christian? It has been common for historians to refer to Constantine's "conversion of 312" (e.g., Barnes 1985). Other historians have been scornful of any suggestion that Constantine ever became a Christian (Burckhardt 1956; Kee 1982). If we bear in mind our discussion of early Christian conversion, we can, I think, attribute to Constantine a conversion that to him and the ecclesiastical authorities appeared genuine. But this conversion was late in his reign, not early. Constantine's conversion was not when he had a "moment of psychological conviction" (Barnes 1981:43); rather, it was when he, near life's end, submitted himself to the journey of change prescribed by the traditions of the church.

As we have seen, conversion to Christianity involved a change of a person's belief, belonging, and behavior, in the course of which there might be a strong religious experience. As to Constantine's beliefs, immediately after his decisive battle in 312 Constantine was "instructed" in the rudiments of Christian belief. But Constantine evidently decided not to become a catechumen. So his religious education was unsystematic, and his "reading of the inspired writings" was evidently fitful and self-guided (*VC* 1.32). We can imagine Constantine protesting, "Cannot Caesar decide what he will read?" Although self-taught, Constantine was able to discourse learnedly about Christianity. His *Oration to the Assembly of Saints*, which may date from 325, is a sample of his eloquently expressed belief. "We have," he insisted, "received no aid from human instruction" (*Oration* 11).[3] It was not until later that Constantine was catechized in the beliefs of the church.

How about Constantine's sense of belonging? This also was slow to change. As early as 314, Constantine addressed the bishops as "beloved brethren"; some time later he aligned himself with the bishops as "your fellow servant" (Coleman-Norton 1966:1.59–61; *VC* 3.12). And yet Constantine knew that he did not fully belong among the believers. In his *Oration* he contrasted himself as an outsider to his audience of Christian initiates. His language was defensive. And this is

not surprising. Constantine, who had not become a catechumen, to say nothing of a baptized Christian, could not attend
the church's services. On Sundays he did not gather with the
faithful for the corporate celebration of the eucharist;
instead he engaged, in his palace, in "solitary converse with
his God" (*VC* 4.22). Constantine clearly did not fully belong
among the Christians.

As to behavior, one wonders how Constantine would have
responded to the teachings that the catechists typically
imparted to their catechumens. Constantine was of course
emperor, and as such he behaved as emperors were wont to
do. At times he deferred to Christian sensibilities, as when
he outlawed the punishment of branding of convicted crimi-
nals on the face "which has been made in the likeness of
celestial beauty" (Pharr 1952; *Codex Theodosianus* [*CT*]
9.40.2). And yet Constantine was hardly squeamish. By the
end of his reign, the use of torture had increased markedly
and the number of capital crimes had risen to over six hundred (MacMullen 1990:213). Furthermore, Constantine's
own reflexes were brutal. In 325, the year before he ordered
the killing of his son and his wife, Constantine protested in
his *Oration* (26): "Surely all men know that the holy service
in which these hands have been employed has originated in
pure and genuine faith towards God." Some, comparing his
behavior with the teaching and traditions of the church,
might have wondered.

Why had Constantine been reluctant to become a
Christian at an earlier stage, by ordinary means? We read
that Constantine was "hesitant, of two minds" (*VC* 4.62), and
it is not hard to see why. On the one hand, there is
Constantine's apparently sincere interest in the Christian
faith. Constantine was grateful to God for evidently vindicat-
ing his cause through triumphs in battle. The prayer that he
prescribed for his soldiers thanked God that "by thee we
have gained victories, by thee we are superior to our enemies" (Coleman-Norton 1966:1.88). And Constantine wanted to serve the God of his victories as best he could. But the
early Christian requirement that conversion involve change,

as well as the rituals that articulated this change, would
have given pause to any emperor. An emperor as intellectu-
ally independent as Constantine might have been able to
accept being tutored in orthodox belief. But the Christian
notions of behavior were difficult: for example, their disap-
proval of ostentatious clothing, including purple, or their dis-
avowal of violence and killing. Would Constantine really want
catechists to superintend him as he learned to care for the
poor and visit the sick, and to assess his lifestyle? The
Christian rituals about which Constantine may have heard,
via leaks in the "discipline of the secret" (*disciplina
arcani*), were also forbidding—exorcistic rituals that hissed
in the face and baptismal rites that immersed were scary,
leveling, even life-threatening.

## Conversion *In Extremis*

So throughout two decades of his reign, Constantine offered
the world a new possibility of an unbaptized, uncatechized
person who nevertheless somehow was a Christian—a
Christian lord who had not bowed his knees to the Lord of
the Christians. Only in 337, when he sensed that he was ill
and might not recover, did Constantine approach the
churchmen to become a Christian in the accepted manner
(*VC* 4.61–62).[4] Only then do we find him "kneeling" on the
pavement and confessing his sins. Thereupon "for the first
time" he received the laying-on of hands and was admitted
to prayers. With this ceremony, Constantine, in the twilight
of his life, became a catechumen (Batiffol 1913:264). It does
not appear that his catechetical regimen was onerous or long
in duration. Indeed, considering the state of Constantine's
health, it could not have been. Constantine informed the
bishops that he had long "thirsted and prayed that [he]
might receive the salvation which is in God... [and] be num-
bered henceforth among the flock of the people of God." No
longer did he want to be limited to praying on his own.
Constantine wanted to belong and to "share within the con-
gregation in the prayers alongside all the others."
Constantine was even willing to alter his behavior: "I shall

now impose upon myself rules of life which are worthy of God." The churchmen did some final teaching in "all the necessary injunctions," whereupon they initiated Constantine according to "the prescribed rites" ( evidently of exorcism, baptism, anointing). At life's end Constantine thus was "reborn and initiated." The rites were, as they were meant to be, a powerful experience for Constantine, who was "renewed and filled with divine light… and astonished at the clear manifestation of the divine power."

We do not know to what extent this conversion process changed Constantine's beliefs. How about his behavior? Eusebius informs us only that Constantine "resolved never to come in contact with purple again" (*VC* 4.62). Given the shortness of his life expectancy, that may not have been too onerous.[5] Most portentously for the future, after his initiation Constantine *belonged*. Eusebius thought it worth reporting that at the Pentecost celebrations that were then under way "the Emperor was admitted to all these rites" (4.64). Hitherto the baptismal confession—the *sacramentum*—had got people in trouble with the emperor. Now the emperor himself had taken the *sacramentum*, with all of the possibilities and ambiguities that this offered.

It is impressive that the church leaders required Constantine to go through all this. For many years they, faced with a potential recruit of no less power and eminence than the emperor—and an emperor who was already favoring the church in many ways—nevertheless held him at arm's length. And when they eventually received him, they did so only on the condition that he go through the well-tried conversion processes of the church. We do not know what postbaptismal teaching (mystagogy) Constantine received. But apart from that, it is striking that Constantine's journey of conversion, rushed and truncated though it was, had all the requisite stages. It is also noteworthy that his delaying of conversion established a pattern of dithering and deathbed conversion (baptism called "clinical" because it took place in bed [*kline*]) that would be common until infant baptism became normal practice.

## Broadening Christianity's Attraction:
## Inducement and Compulsion

The conversion of the emperor was to have lasting effects upon the church. Of course, for half a century prior to Constantine, things had been changing for many Christians. After the ending of the persecution of Galerius in 258, there was a period of exceptional peace for most Christians. In some areas church membership increased rapidly. There is evidence that Christians, no longer a beleaguered minority, were becoming a recognized part of the local landscape (Mitchell 1993; Lepelley 1984). Wealthy people, including decurions, members of the local aristocracy, were finding their place in the churches (Wischmeyer 1992). What was conversion like for these recruits? One of these, Phileas of Thmouis in Upper Egypt, reportedly had enough wealth, according to his inquisitor, "that you could feed and take care not only of yourself but of the whole city." But Phileas remained firm in his nonconformity. Even when subjected to severe pressure, he refused to swear an oath: "It is not permitted to us to swear. For the holy divine scripture declares, 'Let your Yes be Yes and your No, No'"; and he took every opportunity to inform his persecutors about the work and teaching of Jesus (*Acts of Phileas* 5, 11). Phileas was martyred for his stubbornness. He may have been exceptional. One wonders whether the churches' prescribed journey of conversion changed the growing numbers of new Christians as much as their advent changed the churches.

All of these realities became more pronounced after Constantine's victory. Except for a brief period in the 360s, the emperors were Christian of one flavor or another. Some of these, such as Constantine himself, were determined not to engage in any form of religious coercion. In the 320s he observed: "It is one thing voluntarily to undertake the conflict for immortality, another to compel others to do so from the fear of punishment" (*VC* 2.60).

Nevertheless, as the fourth century progressed, Constantine and his successors proffered powerful incentives for conversion to Christianity. By the century's end, patterns of pressure—Sir Herbert Butterfield (1949:135) called them "inducement and compulsion"—were well developed, and these contributed much to the rapid growth of the churches. The inducements were far-reaching: imperially conferred benefits for church leaders, including immunity from onerous public duties; the enrichment of churches; the advancement of the careers of civil servants who had become Christian; and the respectability that adherence to the emperor's religion now entailed. Compulsion was slower to develop. Hints of it were found as early as the 340s, when an imperial edict applied to pagan worship the word that hitherto had been used for Christians—*superstitio*, denoting an intolerable deviation from society's norms of behavior. In 380 the orthodox authorities banned "heretical" Christian groups from public acts of worship; in 392 they outlawed the many who continued to adhere to some form of paganism from engaging in public worship (*CT* 16.10.2; 16.1.2; *Constitutiones Sirmondianae* [*CS*] 12). It was increasingly difficult for known pagans to get work in an imperial establishment; in 416 an imperial edict specified that only professing Christians could be hired by the imperial armies and civil service; and in 529 an edict of Justinian made conversion—including the baptism of all infants—compulsory (*CT* 16.19.21; *Codex Iustinianus* [*CI*] 1.11.10). The result of these measures was of course a myriad of conversions. Augustine reported that, in Hippo, many people—"schismatics," no doubt—had been converted to "Catholic unity by the fear of the imperial laws" (*Ep* 93). Not until Justinian was there any legal compulsion for pagans to join the church. But long before that the pagans felt the pressure, not least of local lords imposing their own often new-found religious allegiance on their neighbors. "For long," Augustine commented, "Christians did not dare answer a pagan; now, thank God, it is a crime to remain a pagan" (*Enarr in Ps* 34/2.13). Ambrose and Augustine both reported that fewer miraculous events were taking place than earlier in the church's history (Ambrose, *De Sacramentis* 2.15; Augustine, *Sermon* 88.3). With Christians thoroughly in control, God's power—to which pre-Constantinian Christians had pointed as a vindication of their cause—was evidently less necessary.[6]

## The Transformation of the Catechumenate

These developments were bound to change the character of conversion. In some churches, change seems to have happened slowly. The liturgical practices of communities in Egypt and Asia Minor represented by the *Canons of Hippolytus* and the *Testamentum Domini* continued to have catechism, scrutinies of behavior, and baptism largely in keeping with the practices of the *Apostolic Tradition*. In the 380s in Syria, the community of the *Apostolic Constitutions* still had a functioning catechumenate in the traditional mold, which the community assumed would last for three years, except for a candidate who was "diligent" and had "a goodwill for his business" (8.32).

But in many places change was taking place rapidly, at times as a result of a transformation in the catechumenate itself. As the fourth century proceeded, in many places admission to the catechumenate, which had been difficult, became routinized. In upper Egypt, a papyrus form letter has survived recommending a person for admission to the catechumenate, with a blank for the candidate's name (Judge 1977:81); all candidates are alike! Augustine records how he, as a child, became a catechumen. As an infant child of Christian parents, he was brought to a priest who gave him the salt of exorcism to taste and signed him with the cross; presumably the priest also conferred the laying on of hands. Augustine was now a catechumen and like other catechumens was "already a believer" (*Confessions* 1.11.17). Augustine and other catechumens like him had now entered Stage 2 of their journey of initiation (for Augustine himself, Stage 1—evangelization—was very short indeed). As in the days before Constantine, they could now attend Sunday Bible readings and sermons, although they had to leave the assembly before the prayers and the eucharist. But this group of catechumens was vastly larger and less disciplined—indeed, less catechized—than they had been a century earlier.

For many of the catechumens, Stage 2 was less a journey than an extended period of aimless milling about—attending church if they found it convenient, listening if they chose, behaving as they wished. It took an act of will for them to continue on their journey of conversion; they had to "give in their names" and to join those actively seeking baptism. If they did so, they, in Stage 3, would be members of a group—variously called *competentes, electi, photizomenoi*—who for a period of time received daily teaching. In Alexandria and Leo's Rome, this lasted forty days; in Chrysostom's Antioch it lasted thirty days; in Cyril's Jerusalem it filled "the eight weeks of Lent."[7] For most candidates, this period of effective teaching was much shorter than it had been before Constantine. In a shorter catechumenate, less could be taught; there could be less supervising of the candidates' progress, less encouraging and modeling by the sponsors. Stage 3, as in the third century, culminated in the baptismal rites of the Easter vigil.

So words can deceive: most fourth-century catechumens were not being catechized, except in the most general sense that they were able to go to sermons if they wished. Instead, they were the large, amorphous group of unbaptized "Christians" hesitating and temporizing, deferring the time when they would be willing to submit themselves to the rigors of conversion. Some, like Constantine, would do so only at death's door, when they would receive "clinical baptism."

To reach these ditherers, pastors and theologians developed a special genre of sermon, containing threat and appeal. Don't delay, pleaded Gregory of Nazianzus in Asia Minor. Enroll as a candidate for baptism "while thy tongue is not stammering or parched... before there is a struggle between the man who would baptize thee and the man who seeks thy money." Gregory addressed his listeners' hesitations and excuses, which provide an interesting perspective on popular—in part accurate, in part out-of-date—perceptions of conversion: converts would have to relinquish involvement in the "stain" of public affairs; they would be cut off from "the pleasures of life"; they might have to yield their concern for status—

to be baptized by a bishop or not "to be with a poor man"; they would have to overcome their fear of "the medicine of exorcism... [and] its length." To those who were willing to be converted, Gregory offered himself as "the director of your soul" (*Oratio* 40).[8] Those who agreed to invitations such as Gregory's were then subjected to initiatory liturgies of increasing solemnity and theatricality. Fourth-century writers dwelt at length on their "awesome" and "hair-raising" qualities. Were these rites, as E. J. Yarnold has wondered, increasingly indebted to pagan mystery rites (1971:55–62)? And were they, as Paul Bradshaw has speculated, designed to be a means of producing—at a time when floods of candidates were coming for initiation—"a powerful emotional and psychological impression upon the candidates in the hope of bringing about their conversion" (Bradshaw, forthcoming)?

Whatever the motivation of the converts, it is clear that by the second half of the fourth century we have entered a new era in church history. Christianity has come to be the religion by royal appointment, and its numbers—and its place in society—were changing rapidly. Membership in the Christian church was now attractive in new ways, and it held out new opportunities for Christian influence. A few Christians publicly expressed hesitations with the newly developing order, but very few.[9] Christendom—a Christian civilization with common understandings of belief, belonging, and behavior, and with widely shared forms of religious experience—was dawning. And, as we will see, as a result of the conversion of the emperor the meaning of conversion itself would change.

# 5

# Catechizing the Masses: Cyril and Chrysostom

In the fourth century, catechism took on a new, public significance. It was bound to. The number of baptismal candidates was growing; in Antioch, a major city, in the 390s there could be as many as a thousand per year (Piédagnel 1990:43). This presented the church's leaders with a major opportunity—of addressing the interested pagans and catechumens from infancy, forming them spiritually and practically so that they, after their baptisms, would be authentically converted. In the fourth century a number of significant catechists emerged. Let us listen to two of them—Cyril and John Chrysostom—and through them get a glimpse of what conversion meant in two fourth-century churches—Jerusalem and Antioch.[1]

### Cyril: Making Jerusalem Converts
### Invincible Against Heresy

We begin with Jerusalem, where in 348 the presbyter (later bishop) Cyril gave a series of catechetical lectures. Many of these may still have been in his repertoire in the early 380s, when the observant traveler Egeria listened so appreciatively to his teaching (*Travels* 45.1–46.6). Cyril's teaching began, according to Egeria, at the beginning of Lent when catechumens (Stage 2 people) gave in their names. One by one they came with their sponsors before Cyril, who asked the sponsors: "Is this person leading a good life? Does he respect his parents? Is he a drunkard or a boaster?" These questions may seem somewhat undemanding by the standards of the *Apostolic Tradition*, which had inquired about the candidates' relations to employers and whether their jobs required idolatry or killing. But Egeria reported that the questions were enough to send some candidates away. Those who passed the examination, however, were immediately exorcised and then admitted to Stage 3, an intensive course of prebaptismal teaching. Every weekday morning for eight weeks, those about to be illumined (*photizomenoi*) gathered in a circle about Cyril for a three-hour session; to these gatherings any of the baptized faithful could come. But of course, Egeria emphasized, the Stage 2 catechumens must not know the content of the catechism.

What did Cyril teach? Egeria's reports from the 380s are sketchy and appear somewhat different from Cyril's nineteen written catechisms that date from thirty years earlier. According to Egeria, Cyril spent forty days "going through the whole Bible, beginning with Genesis," dealing with its literal and spiritual meanings, thereby building up the candidates' sense of Christian belonging by introducing them to the narratives of the Christian tradition. In the sixth and seventh weeks Cyril concentrated his attention on the beliefs of Christianity; article by article he explained the Creed. At the beginning of the Easter Week—the eighth week—one by one the candidates with their sponsors went to Cyril to recite the Creed. If they got through this satisfactorily, their week was full of intense catechizing and religious activity, which culminated in the Easter vigil in which the candidates were baptized and for the first time took part in the eucharist. In the week following Easter the newly baptized believers experienced Stage 4; they received final, "mystagogical" catechism on five days, during which time they received instruction about the sacraments of baptism and the eucharist. Henceforth they, as Christians, belonged.

The surviving texts of Cyril's nineteen catechetical lectures are useful in elucidating his strategy and his priorities. In his introductory catechetical address (*Procatechesis*) Cyril welcomed the candidates into "the vestibule of the king's palace." The coming weeks would be a special time for the candidates, but already they had "an odor of blessedness." But Cyril recognized that, even though the candidates had already survived a scrutiny of their behavior, some of them had probably come for mixed motives. A man may wish to court a woman; a slave may wish to please his master, or a friend his friend. Cyril accepted all this; it was a "bait for the hook" (*Procat* 1, 5). On the days following this introductory lecture, the catechism proper began. If Cyril in 348 was teaching his way through the Bible, his lectures have not survived. Instead, the heart of his extant catechetical lectures dealt with belief. He was concerned to make his charges "invincible against every heretical attempt," so he carefully rehearsed the tenets and shortcomings of the various erroneous options that were circulating in the mid–fourth-century East (*Procat* 10; *Cat* 6.12–36). But his main burden was to impart to his candidates a fund of living belief; in thirteen lectures he elucidated the Apostles' Creed, clause by clause.

### Conversion: Forsaking the Little Things

Cyril was exhaustive in his treatment of orthodox belief. But even in his five mystagogic lectures he seems to have had little to say about belonging.[2] He gave implicit recognition that the convert was joining a new family: the waters of baptism were "at once your grave and your Mother" (*Cat* 20.4). But Cyril said little about a new sense of identity that the baptizand would have. Perhaps the Jerusalem setting militated against this. From Egeria and Cyril it is hard to find reference to a significant local community of non-Christians; and both were intensely conscious that this was the city, not only of Jesus and his passion, but also of the magnificent buildings of "the Emperor Constantine of blessed memory" (14.22).

Already by the mid–fourth century, in Jerusalem Christianity had the feel of an established religion in which belonging was a matter of course.

About behavior Cyril was rather more forthcoming than he was about belonging. He was concerned about "virtuous practice" as well as "pious doctrine" (4.2). In his first lecture he disarmingly told his candidates that they wouldn't have to change much: "Little are the things which thou art forsaking" (1.5). But he then proceeded to indicate that there were indeed areas in which the behavior of Christians should be become distinctive. Christians must forgive others, abstain from "backbiting," and honor their parents. They should also attend church regularly, after baptism as well as "now when diligent attendance is required of thee by the clergy" (1.6). About espousing a simpler lifestyle, Cyril, unlike Cyprian, had nothing to say. Similarly, his catechesis, unlike the church orders following the *Apostolic Tradition*, did not refer to military service. Cyril did quote Matthew 5:48 ("Be perfect as your heavenly Father is perfect"), but not to admonish his hearers to love their enemies; he was concerned only to emphasize that God was perfect (6.8). About the duty to care for the poor Cyril had more to say. The candidates should not despise wealth, as he said some heretical groups were doing, for without wealth they could not respond to Jesus' call to feed the hungry. So, Cyril commented, "a man may even be justified by money" (8.6). But sharing with the poor was nothing less than a condition of eternal felicity. About the famous passage of Matthew 25:31ff ("I was hungry and you fed me…") Cyril commented: "there is no need of allegory…. These things, if thou do, thou shalt reign with him; but if thou do them not, thou shalt be condemned" (15.26).

The newly baptized, Cyril emphasized, could behave badly. "The Lord Jesus Christ," he told the neophytes, "[could be] blasphemed through thee." In this way Cyril betrayed an implicit missionary concern. But he was also convinced that the new Christians could be true to their new identity: "Thou art called a Christian: be tender of the name." As such they should "let their good works shine before men" so that people might glorify the Father (10.20). So there was, in Cyril's catechesis, a concern that the behavior of his candidates change. But Cyril did not present his catechumens with the Isaiah/Micah vision, so common in Origen and other earlier writers, of the church as a society in which swords were beaten into ploughshares. No, Cyril's priorities were clear. He was concerned about purity of belief, to which he devoted at least twenty times the attention he gave to changed behavior. His teaching against "the brood of heretics" was vastly more practical, more "how-to-do-it," than his much briefer teachings on behavior could be (16.4–11). For Cyril, conversion meant, above all, believing the right things.

## Chrysostom: Burial and
## Resurrection in Missionary Antioch

In Antioch, a hundred miles to the north of Jerusalem, in the 380s John Chrysostom was providing another fourth-century approach to conversion. Antioch, unlike Jerusalem, was a city in which Christianity was surrounded by vital religious options; both Judaism and paganism were flourishing, and were active rivals to orthodox Christianity (Meeks and Wilken 1978). So it is not surprising that Chrysostom showed a much keener sense of the conflict and change involved in conversion than Cyril did. The Christian church in Antioch was in a missionary situation, in active contention with the ways and understandings of the surrounding culture. "Put away from you all you have done up to now," he urged his baptismal candidates, "and prove with all your heart that you are through with the past" (*Baptismal Instructions* 1.18).

In his church in Antioch Chrysostom was a leading catechist. Twelve of his homilies have survived from this period: seven of these he gave in Stage 3 during the weeks prior to baptism, and five (the so-called mystagogic catecheses) he addressed to the newly baptized believers in Stage 4. The period of prebaptismal instruction was a time of spiritual struggle as well as of learning; it was "like the practice and bodily exercise in some wrestling school" (9.29). Daily the candidates came for an instruction, after which exorcists cleansed their minds with "frightening and horrible words," using an "awful formula" (2.12). Accompanying them step-by-step were their sponsors, "encouraging, counseling, and correcting those for whom they go surety" (2.15). As the candidates' minds were instructed and Satan's many-faceted hold was broken, they were being prepared for the climactic rituals in the Easter vigil. Chrysostom—unlike some of his contemporary catechists—was candid and detailed in his description of the baptismal rites: after the candidates were disrobed, anointed, and immersed, their new family rushed to receive them:

> As soon as they come forth from the sacred waters, all who are present embrace them, greet them, kiss them, rejoice with them, and congratulate them, because those who were heretofore slaves and captives have suddenly become free men and sons and have been invited to... the awesome table (2.27).

Chrysostom was passionately convinced that the believer emerging from the waters was "a different man" who has experienced a vast change (2.25). He marshaled his considerable rhetorical powers to describe this change: it was not only a liberation of captives; for the new believers it was a matter of nothing less than "burial and resurrection" (2.11). The Christians in their voluntary new birth had concluded a pact—a "contract of renunciation and attachment"—with God (2.17). Henceforth they would be committed to a changed life.

### Strict Dogmas for Citizens of Another State

The expressions of this changed life that Chrysostom offered to the apprentice Christians in Antioch came in categories that are by now familiar to us. The new Christians would be committed to orthodox belief, especially with regard to the Trinity: they would be vigilant against the errors of the

Arians and the Sabellians. Moreover, their attitude to the "dogmas of the church" would be marked by "strictness" (1.20–25). Christians would ponder the stories of the faithful—Abraham, Paul, Cornelius—who would be models for their thought and action. But Chrysostom, at least in his surviving baptismal instructions, did not seem to be primarily concerned to implant the beliefs and narratives of the Christian faith in the minds of his charges. Unlike Cyril in Jerusalem, Chrysostom evidenced concerns that were less doctrinal than missionary and pastoral.

Chrysostom therefore gave considerable attention to the quality of belonging that the Christian convert would experience. The belonging was, of course, to Jesus Christ. The new believer, though uncomely and deformed, had entered into a "spiritual marriage" with Christ her Bridegroom, through whom she would be purified and made beautiful (1.11). The belonging was also to a new society, the church. This was both a "spiritual army" and a family. Its members were brothers and sisters of one another and also "citizens of the church" (3.5). Chrysostom did not catechize his candidates in the consequences of their being "citizens of another state" (4.29); one wonders what impact upon the believer he would have foreseen of a solidarity that superseded race and place. At another level of belonging—the commitment of believers to each other "for we are members one of another"—Chrysostom was explicit. When other Christians fall prey to "laxity," when they succumb to the snares of "worldly amusement," the believers are to "take up the task of your brother's salvation" by reproving them, encouraging them back to the Christian way of solidarity in discipline (6.15, 18).

### Behavior: Choosing a New and Different Form of Life

It was, however, on matters of Christian behavior that Chrysostom especially lectured his class of converts. Because they had "chosen henceforth a new and different form of life," the new Christians must manifest comprehensive change (4.24). In a no doubt unintentional echo of Cyprian's words, Chrysostom noted of the new believers:

> He who yesterday and the day before spent his time in luxurious and gluttonous living, suddenly embraces a life of self-control and simplicity…. He who was formerly incontinent and consumed with the pleasures of their life suddenly rises above his passions and… pursues the life of temperance and chastity (4.13).

Conversion, Chrysostom was convinced, must involve people at every level of their lives. It must challenge and erase their bad habits and offer them new dimensions of freedom. Of the four areas of addiction and compulsion that Justin had pointed to in second-century Rome (1 *Apol* 14), Chrysostom was more sensitive to some than to others. Chrysostom was deeply concerned at the hold that the occult—omens, charms, and incantations—had upon people (12.53). But in these homilies he gave surprisingly little attention to dangers of the flesh, except for his special distaste for female adornment: "there is nothing more disgusting," he commented, "than a suspiciously beautiful face" (12.42). As for wealth, Chrysostom was eloquent on its capacity to become addictive: it "often takes those who have a passion for it and surrounds them with dangers they cannot resist" (8.12). Chrysostom urged the apprentice Christians to embrace "self-control and simplicity" (4.13) and to find freedom not least through the spiritual discipline of almsgiving; he did not catechize them on possible mechanisms for economic redistribution within the church (7.27). As to enemies, one was to seek reconciliation with them (1.41); but this, unlike the *Apostolic Tradition*, did not cause Chrysostom to query Christian participation in the legions or in killing. Chrysostom was categorical (was he responding to other Christians who, following an earlier tradition, disagreed with him? [Hornus 1980:161–70]): "Military service presents no hindrance to virtue for the man who is willing to be sober." The real issue for the soldier, as for the civilian, was sobriety of speech and lifestyle (7.28; 8.17).

Chrysostom's passion for changed behavior overflowed when he discussed two areas in which addiction was notably present—the hippodrome and the oath. It was not simply that the chariot races and spectacles in the hippodrome were a rival attraction to attendance at church ("our congregations are shrinking" [6.1]). Lawless and unbridled, the spectacles were embodiments of the pomp of Satan (12.52), infinitely seductive and corrupting of the Christian's soul.

### Breaking the Addictive Power of Oath Taking

Even worse than the attraction to the hippodrome was the habit of swearing oaths: "Above all," said Chrysostom, "teach your tongues to be clean in the matter of oaths" (1.42). Chrysostom acknowledged that not all Christians agreed with him, but this was no small matter. He viewed it as so important that Christians should refuse to swear at all ("I do not speak only of perjured oaths but even of true oaths" [9.39]) that he returned to the matter in no fewer than five of his twelve lectures. Why was this so important to him? Chrysostom observed that Christians, like others in Antioch, swore oaths in the course of daily life habitually, virtually automatically.

> Whether we are buying vegetables and arguing over two obols or are threatening our servants in our anger, we always call on God as our witness.... When you are talking about goods for sale and money and insignificant things, you drag in the King of heaven and Lord of angels to be your witness (9.45).

Like Christian theologians before him, Chrysostom found this objectionable (Kreider 1997). Jesus had commanded his followers not to swear at all, and "if he has commanded it, we must obey and must not use this or that man [who swears] as an excuse" (9.41). For Chrysostom, swearing was "a destructive drug, a bane and a danger, a hidden wound, a sore unseen, an obscure ulcer" that led people to spiritual death. Sooner or later they would inevitably swear something unlawful, in which case they would be spiritually destroyed either by reneging on the oath (perjury) or by doing an unlawful deed (10.18). But how could Christians avoid swearing, which for so many people had become habitual? In a remarkable passage, Chrysostom elaborated a six-step method for unlearning an ingrained habit. To stop swearing, Chrysostom urged his catechumens to ask others to remind them; to be alert to the power of habit; to make conscious decisions to change over to a good habit; to reproach others when they swore oaths; to set a time limit—for example, ten days—for discarding the habit; and, finally, to fine themselves monetarily if they hadn't corrected the fault within the allotted time (9.42–46). To check on how his catechumens were progressing in their efforts to repent, he returned to the issue in his next homily: "Did you cleanse your tongue from this grievous sin?" (10.2). If behavior were to change as well as belief and belonging, if the catechumens were to root out implanted habits, other catechists must have used methods such as Chrysostom's; but this is the only instance that I am aware of in the ancient literature of a catechist systematically working at techniques to convert the behavior of his catechumens.

Chrysostom's vision of conversion was an exalted one—more powerful and life encompassing than that of Cyril. Christians, he was convinced, were freed by God through catechism and awesome rite to enter a new world of solidarity and transformed behavior. But, by pre-Constantinian standards, the configuration of conversion had discernibly changed. Chrysostom's teaching was rooted in a broad swathe of scripture, much broader, for example, than Ambrose's catechism in Milan, which dealt with "right conduct" on the basis of "the lives of the patriarchs... [and] the precepts of the Proverbs" (Ambrose, *De Mysteriis* 1.1). Chrysostom's appeal to the witness of exemplary role models—Abraham, Cornelius, and Paul—was also broader than Ambrose's (Ferguson, forthcoming). But it is striking that Chrysostom rarely referred to Jesus Christ as teacher or example. This may have been because Chrysostom thought it was the monks whose lifestyle enacted the lesson of Jesus' way, which was too demanding for ordinary Christians (8.3). It may also have reflected a widespread reluctance, evident among many orthodox fourth-century writers, to refer to the example of Jesus; in their reaction to the arguments of the Arians they had come to see the appeal to Jesus as theologically suspect (Wilken 1995:126–27).

It is also notable that Chrysostom's social strategy had less to do with the corporate life of the church than with the lives of individual believers. He did not, unlike many earlier theologians, pass on to his candidates Isaiah/Micah's "swords into ploughshares" passage as a defining text for the church.[3] Nor did he lecture his candidates about the possibilities of the church as an addiction-free society; but he held forth the ideal of individual Christians who, strengthened by God's help, would live with discipline and sobriety in their daily tasks. For Chrysostom, it was through the individual, more than through the Christian community, that God's light would shine. The Christian individual lived in ways—"one hastening to work with his hands, another hurrying to his military post, and still another to his post with the government"—that would with inner piety and outer discipline enable the empire to function (8.16–17).

# 6

# Attracting the Recalcitrant: Augustine and Volusian

### Augustine the Converter

The most famous early Christian conversion was that of Augustine. Scholars debate how many conversions he had, and they discuss at length the spiritual, psychological, and ritual dimensions of his journey (Madec 1986; Geerlings 1987; Finn 1997:chap. 9). To enrich this discussion, Augustine left his wonderfully illuminating *Confessions*. But my focus will not be on Augustine as convert; it will be on the less celebrated story of Augustine the converter. Augustine was bishop of Hippo in North Africa for thirty-four years, from 396 to 430. During this time, "orthodox" Catholic Christianity decisively established itself as the religion of the imperial establishment, and through this its influence spread into every town. Augustine reflected on the results of this Christianization: "In this city there are many houses in which there is not even a single pagan, nor a single house in which there is not a Christian" (*Sermon* 302.19). In this process of conversion, Augustine played a role that was vital locally, but he also left his impact upon the history of Christendom as a whole.[1]

When Augustine became bishop in 396, recently passed imperial laws had already begun to ease the expansion of Christianity. At first, Augustine had doubted whether coercion could bring genuine change. In his *Confessions* he recalled how, in his boyhood, he had learned the Latin language, which delighted him so much: "I learnt Latin without the threat of punishment from anyone forcing me to learn it. My own heart constrained me.... This experience sufficiently illuminates the truth that free curiosity has greater power to stimulate learning than rigorous coercion" (*Confessions* 1.14.23). His early writings indicate that he had similar views on religious coercion (*Retractions* 2.31). But North Africa was a hard world. As a bishop, Augustine was involved in struggles with religious rivals—especially "schismatic" Donatists and pagans. These struggles at times also involved him in contests with local power brokers for influence and dominance. So before long Augustine became an active participant in the Christianization, by favor, fiat, and force, of North Africans and their society.

Augustine's understanding of his role was an exalted one. Certain, like his predecessor Cyprian, that there was "no salvation outside the Church," Augustine saw himself as a rescuer of souls. Augustine was concerned to build a church that was as comprehensive and faithful as possible—that would be orthodox in its belief, obedient in its behavior, and universal in its "Catholic unity" (*Ep* 93). This required him lovingly to apply discipline. Error, he was convinced, could have no rights. He was not eager for Christians to engage in acts of vandalism against pagan shrines; acts of destruction and the redeployment of buildings should be left to the duly constituted authorities (Lepelley 1979:353). Nevertheless, pagan shrines, such as that of the god of strength, Hercules, could be subjected to a symbolic, humiliating, desecrating "shaving" (MacMullen 1997:51). Augustine's self-image as he presided over the Christianization of Africa was that of the attentive surgeon: "He cuts to heal" (*Enarr in Ps* 34.2.13). And yet Augustine remained aware that it was easier to deprive pagans of their public rights than it was to bring about Christian conversion: "It is easier to close temples than it is to close people's hearts to the idols" (*Ep* 232).

Augustine, as a missionary pastor, was profoundly concerned that people be converted in the fullest sense of the word.

### The Attraction and Repulsion of the Christians' Behavior

So how could Christianity attract the pagans? As we will see, Augustine engaged in respectful, pastorally sensitive, private correspondence with pagan aristocrats. But in his public role, Augustine of course was unable to appeal directly to the pagans. They, in keeping with Christian tradition, were not allowed into the Christian assemblies to hear his sermons.[2] So witness had to be indirect. Augustine was clear-eyed in his awareness that inducement and compulsion attracted people to the church. A man might make an initial approach to the church "to derive some benefit from men whom he thinks he could not otherwise please, or to escape some injury at the hands of men whose displeasure or enmity he dreads" (*First Catechetical Instruction* 5.9).[3] The role of the *potentiores*—landowners, powerful local men—could be useful in converting their retainers: "If such a proprietor became a Christian, no one would remain a pagan" (*Enarr in Ps* 54.13). Christian poor relief, so central to the church's tradition, also could attract pagans to explore membership (Van der Meer 1961:30).

The best way of drawing pagans to faith was embedded deeply in Christian tradition—the attractive life of Christian people: "Christ is announced through Christian friends" (*Tract in Ev Ioan* 15.33). But this approach was not working as well as it had done earlier. Whereas Minucius Felix could use the lives of the Christians as evidence of Christianity's truth (*Octavius* 38.6), now pagans could point to the behavior of Christians as evidence of Christianity's fraudulence. Augustine was aware of this. He knew that many Christians were living lives that repelled pagans. So he exhorted his flock to treat pagans well: "When you, a Christian… strip a pagan bare, you prevent his becoming a Christian" (*Sermon* 179.4). Pagans, he observed, looked at Christians and sniffed: "Do you want me to be like that so-and-so and the other one?" (*Sermon* 15.6). Augustine knew that these reactions were at times justified, for there was a host of "depraved persons who in mobs fill the churches in a bodily sense only" (*First Catechetical Instr* 7.12). And yet he repeatedly exhorted Christians new and old to live lives that would be attractive and worthy of imitation—lives that would lure people into beginning the journey of conversion.

### Urging the Catechumens to Be Converted

In Augustine's Hippo, the journey of conversion retained its classical, four-stage form. In his *First Catechetical Instruction* he provides the most comprehensive treatment in the church's first millennium of how an inquirer could best be dealt with in Stage 1. Writing in 405, Augustine advised the deacon Deogratias, who was a catechist, as to how he could most effectively "present the truth, the belief which makes us Christians" in such a way that the inquirer would want to continue the journey by becoming a catechumen (1.1). It was important, Augustine counseled, that the catechist should emphasize love. He must communicate to the inquirer "how much God loves him... so that he might begin to glow with love of him by whom he was first loved, and so might love his neighbor." (4.8). The comportment and the insightful adaptability of the catechists were crucial. Catechists must observe carefully the inquirers who are before them: who are they? what are their educational attainments? what is their physical strength? should they stand or sit as the catechist speaks? what is their motivation? Augustine knew that inquirers came with a variety of motivations—fear and the desire to ingratiate were especially common. Perhaps the biggest challenge, he sensed, was the "apathy" of the inquirer: "it is a hard thing to continue speaking... when we do not see our hearer moved" (13.18).

With these considerations in mind, the catechist was then to present the "truth" and the "precepts" of the Christian faith as persuasively as possible. Central to this presentation was narrative. In keeping with venerable tradition, Augustine's catechist was to present his inquirers with an overview of salvation history. Augustine provided two models of this, the longer of which assumed considerable concentration on the part of the hearer; in unelaborated form it takes sixty minutes to read. More briefly, the catechist was then to spell out the precepts "of a Christian, upright manner of life." Of course the inquirer would find many people "called Christians" who were all the things he was instructed not to be—"drunkards, covetous, extortioners, gamblers, adulterers, fornicators, lovers of shows, wearers of idolatrous charms, soothsayers, astrologers, or diviners employing vain and unholy arts." But, Augustine advised Deogratias, "We should also assure him that he will find many good Christians in the Church." In all of this the catechist should recall that the basic impulse leading to conversion was fear. Fear more than any other motive was likely to have brought the inquirer to see the catechist; and fear, instilled by the catechist, who recounted "the punishments of the wicked... with loathing and horror," would be the most significant impetus in persuading the inquirer to become a catechumen and thereby to begin the journey to become one of Christ's friends (7.11).

If the catechumens, at the end of his introductory session, assented to this initial exposition of Christian belief, a brief ceremony ensued. The catechist signed the inquirers with the sign of the cross and imparted to them "the sacrament of salt" (26.50). Having thus become "catechumens," the inquirers entered Stage 2 of their journey. They were now accounted "Christians" (*Sermon* 97A.3) and were accepted as members of the Christian community in its widest sense. As such they were allowed to attend the readings and sermons that constituted the first part of the Sunday services in the Christian churches, and these provided a wide-ranging if unsystematic catechism for them if they were attentive. Augustine's sermons on John's Gospel, for example, would have introduced them to Christian doctrine, while his sermons on the Psalms plumbed the depths of Christian spirituality and sensibility (Harmless 1995:chap. 6). But the catechumens were not authentic Christians; they "haven't yet been forgiven, because they are only forgiven in holy baptism" (*Sermon* 97A.3). In this indeterminate state— "Christian" yet unconverted, "catechumen" yet uncatechized— the catechumens could continue for many years. These were Augustine's primary missionary target. Every year, as the Lenten season approached, Augustine preached sermons urging the catechumens to stop temporizing and present themselves for baptism. "Look, it's Easter time, put your name down for baptism. If the festival doesn't get you excited, at least let curiosity lead you on" (*Sermon* 132.1). Augustine knew their excuses: "This is the thing that kills many people, when they say, 'Tomorrow, tomorrow,' and suddenly the door is shut" (*Sermon* 82.14). Augustine, fearful of his own responsibility for the salvation of souls, appealed to a favorite text (Sirach 5:8) to terrify the catechumens into taking the next steps of faith.

> You in particular, you bad procrastinator with your bad longing for tomorrow, listen to the Lord speaking, listen to holy scripture preaching.... "Do not be slow to turn to the Lord, nor put it off from day to day. For suddenly his wrath will come, and at the time for vengeance he will destroy you." Did I write that? Can I cross it out? If I cross it out, I'm afraid of being crossed out myself.... I'm compelled to preach it. In terror I aim to terrify. Be afraid with me in order to rejoice with me. Do not be slow to turn to the Lord (*Sermon* 40.5).

Year after year some catechumens turned a deaf ear to such appeals, but others responded. Early in Lent they gave in their names and submitted themselves for systematic preparation for baptism.

Augustine's converts thus entered Stage 3 of their journey of conversion. No longer were they catechumens; for a few weeks they were now *competentes*, "people asking together" (*Sermon* 216). According to long tradition, this was a time in which the candidates, in company with their sponsors (the "parents of rebirth"), attended frequent sessions preparing them for change in their beliefs, behavior, and sense of belonging. It was a time of "wrestling" in a spiritual stadium in which they were repeatedly exorcized. Two weeks before Easter they were given the Creed, which they memorized so they could "recite [it] in bed… [and] think about [it] in the streets" (*Sermon* 215). A week later they were taught the Lord's Prayer. And through the entire catechetical process, their priorities and conduct were to change. "You used to be conformed to the world's patterns; now be reformed to God's" (*Sermon* 216.4). Out of the stadium, Augustine hoped, there would emerge converted, changed people—authentic "children of God."

## Conversion's Change Must Precede Baptism

For some lay Christians in North Africa, this all seemed over-intense and counterproductive. These people, whom Augustine conceded were "learned in the Scriptures," argued that it was wrong to expect candidates to change their behavior before they were baptized. "They think," Augustine reported, "that the sacrament of baptism should come first; the teaching concerning morals and the life of a Christian should follow afterwards." They justified their position by citing a wide selection of biblical texts. The Ethiopian eunuch, for example, was baptized by the apostle Philip, immediately, without investigation of his lifestyle, without catechism (Acts 8:37). Why not just teach the rule of faith to converts and then baptize them? Afterward, after they are baptized, they could be taught the "precepts of conduct in the hope that they will change their lives for the better" (*Faith and Works* 1.1; 9.14).

Augustine was unpersuaded by this approach, which would be typical of many later Christians. But he took it seriously enough to devote a substantial treatise—*On Faith and Works*—to refute the arguments of its adherents. Augustine, in line with long-hallowed tradition, was convinced that Stage 3 of the conversion process was essential. In part, this was because it was a time of excitement and anticipation:

"What better time is there to teach him how to live a good, Christian life than when he is all anxious and eager to receive this most salutary sacrament [baptism]?" (6.9). Further, the church had always required behavioral change to precede baptism. As in the *Apostolic Tradition*, people in forbidden professions— "prostitutes, actors, or any disreputable person"— must abandon their jobs if they were to be admitted. (Augustine, unlike the *Apostolic Tradition* 16, did not proscribe soldiers that kill or governors who wear purple.) Forms of unacceptable behavior—"drunkenness, avarice, calumny"—should be addressed in the catechists' instructions. Three sins—impurity, idolatry, and homicide—were "mortally sinful" and hence fundamentally incompatible with Christian faith. As always, Augustine was most sensitive to sexual sin: "If there is any sin for which a person should be refused baptism, that sin is adultery." Teaching about both belief and behavior, Augustine was convinced, was essential in baptismal preparation, "for they are mutually interconnected.... [H]e who does not love his neighbor does not love God." John the Baptist's challenge to his baptismal candidates (Luke 3:11f) was ample evidence "that we are to teach those preparing for baptism the principles of Christian morality" (13.19).

### Spiritual Combat and Behavioral Change

So Augustine, his laxist critics to the contrary, perpetuated the traditional regimen of formation for the baptismal candidates. But Augustine seems to have moved some distance toward his critics. On occasion he enunciated a vision of "perfect conversion," based on the Pentecostal community in Jerusalem in Acts 4: "They sold everything they possessed... and distribution was made to each as each had need, and... all had everything in common" (*Sermon* 77.4). But Augustine's sermons are long on exhortation and short on practical attention to forming the *competentes*' Christian character; unlike Chrysostom, he provided little practical instruction for people who were attempting to root out addictive behavior. To be sure, Augustine provided lists of unacceptable forms of behavior.

I have talked rather more than I ought. I have said something that I should not have said, I have laughed more than I ought. I've drunk more than I ought, I've eaten more than I ought, I have enjoyed hearing what I shouldn't have done (*Sermon* 57.11).

A further classification of sins was the Ten Commandments, which Augustine, for the first time in church history, introduced as a basis for a Christian moral code (Lombardo 1988:85n). And scattered through his catechetical homilies are insightful comments on certain profoundly problematic areas of conversion—the hatred of enemies, avarice, lust (Harmless 1995:179, 296).

But how were the *competentes* to cease these forms of behavior? Augustine gave them little "how-to-do-it" help. This was, he said in an introductory talk to the candidates, their responsibility: "We clergy instruct you with sermons; it is up to you to make progress in your conduct" (*Sermon* 219.1). For actual moral instruction, Augustine seems to have relied on the candidates' own efforts and on their sponsors who were to encourage them in virtue, "not by words but by... good behavior" (*Sermon* 132.2).

But for Augustine the main instrument for effecting behavioral conversion in his candidates was not systematic moral formation; it was spiritual combat. No longer did the prebaptismal scrutiny examine the extent to which the candidates have "lived good lives... [or] honored the widows" (*Apostolic Tradition* 20); now the scrutiny's focus was exorcistic (Poque 1966:26–33). Augustine seemed to assume that it was through repeated exorcisms that the candidates might yet change their way of living. These exorcisms were meant to rebuke and repudiate satanic powers; but it was not incidental that they also were a "terrifying experience" for the candidates (Finn 1990:592). Throughout their Lenten journey the clergy would repeatedly invoke the name of Christ and "heap curses" on Satan "appropriate to his vile wickedness," while the candidates penitently stood on ragged fleeces of she-goats. Thus humiliated, the candidates were to respond "by thoroughly scrutinizing and crushing [their] hearts" and by doing battle with Satan "by turning away from him and devoutly renouncing him." It was a person, converted by means of being cleansed, who in turn would behave in a way that converts others: he "goes in pursuit of those who have run away, finds those who have got lost, humbles the proud, feeds the starving, releases those in fetters, gives light to the blind" (*Sermon* 216.6, 11).

In Augustine's Hippo, as elsewhere, Stage 3 of the journey of conversion culminated in the great events of the Easter Vigil. It was then that the fasting and the exorcisms became most intense. After a final, climactic exorcism, the candidates definitively renounced "the devil, his pomps, and his angels" (*Sermon* 215.1). They recited the Creed, which they had memorized in the previous weeks. In anointing and baptism, they were then finally "converted." They were forgiven; their threefold immersion in the font was a "bath of amnesty" (*Sermon* 223.1). They had concluded a "pact" with God to put off the old man and put on the new. They were washed, liberated, enlightened. Reclad in white, they had "become the light of God's marvels and favors" (*Sermon* 120.3). In their journey they had arrived; at long last they belonged. They had become, together with all the faithful, Christ's Body.

> And you, after those fasts, after the hard labors, after the humiliation and the contrition, have now at last come, in the name of Christ, into the Lord's cup, so to say; and there you are on the table, and there you are in the cup. You are this together with us; we all take this together, all drink together, because we all live together (*Sermon* 229.1).

Eight days of mystagogical teaching (Stage 4) remained, in which the catechists explained the meaning of the mysteries—baptism and communion—that the candidates had just experienced.

### A Middle Course for a "Lame" Church

Conversion was a source of joy. On Easter day Augustine welcomed the "infants" who had just become "brothers and sisters... the new offspring of mother Church." But immediately he began to warn them. They should choose carefully which Christians to associate with and which to choose as role models. The neophytes would be surrounded by bogus Christians "for whom the name of 'faithful' is just a mistake" for they are people without a "new manner of life" (*Sermon* 228). Even after baptism, many people were "unwilling to give up their sin, and wanted to do the same things as they used to do before"—tell lies, perjure themselves, fornicate, get drunk. On the other hand, there were rigorist Christians who, prideful in their fear of mingling with sinners, stayed separate from the church and "perish[ed] through heresies and schisms" (*Sermon* 4.14). The new Christians, Augustine advised, should steer a middle course, living a faithful life while mingling with all others—the chaff as well as the wheat—on the "threshing floor" that is the church (*Sermon* 80.8). Nowhere—neither in his instructions to new believers nor elsewhere—did Augustine pick up the early Christian commonplace that Christians had been reborn into membership in a people of peace who, by converting their swords into ploughshares, were fulfilling the famous passage in Isaiah 2:2–4.[4] No, Augustine's convictions and his experience coincided: inner peace was possible; eschatological peace has been promised; but even in the church "there is no peace in this life" (*Enarr in Ps* 45.10; 48.17).

In Hippo there were richly developed rituals of conversion through which large numbers of people came into membership in the church. But Augustine was realistic about their results: "We can't convert the vast majority to a good life, can we?" (*Sermon* 80.8). There were only a "few who walk along the narrow road" (*Sermon* 224.1). Augustine knew of a few Christians who sought to follow Christ seriously—praying for their enemies, distributing their goods to the needy. But to them, behaving in ways that would have seemed normal to Justin or Cyprian, the response of other Christians was the attribution of madness that conventional people habitually make to those who for religious reasons repudiate society's deepest norms: "Why are you acting crazy?

You're going to extremes; aren't other people Christians? This is plain folly; it's lunacy" (*Sermon* 88.12). Augustine was committed to comprehending all these, somehow, in a capacious and therapeutic church, shepherding the few toward greater humility and the many toward greater fidelity.

Augustine recognized realistically that "the church is lame"; he also insisted fiercely that "the application of discipline" was necessary to cause people to improve their behavior (*Sermon* 5.8; *Retractions* 2.31). What Augustine was reluctant to do was to query whether the lameness was in part a result of his kind of discipline. Could anything other than a limping church result from conversions that, to a lesser or greater extent, had been coerced? Nor did Augustine reflect that, in the process, he had been innovating, presiding over a far-reaching alteration in the nature of the church and its relation to the "world." Augustine was confident in stating: "What the soul is in the body, that the Holy Spirit is in the Body of Christ, the Church" (*Sermon* 267.4). One wonders whether he knew a similar text from the second-century *Epistle to Diognetus* (6.1): "What the soul is in the body, that Christians are in the world." For Augustine, a distinctively living Christian church had disappeared, as had the world. For him, a pioneer of Christendom, the church and the world were becoming so intermingled that they were indistinguishable.

### Volusian—A Roman Aristocrat Considers Christianity

To understand the significance of this for the lives of contemporaries, we would need to tell many stories. Fortunately, the sources enable us to tell one. Not surprisingly, the protagonist was an aristocrat; sources do not survive for individual *humiliores*. But aristocratic males were at long last becoming significant in the church, and the story of Rufius Antonius Agrypnius Volusianus (Volusian) shows the inner dynamics of conversion of one of these who became a Christian.[5]

Volusian was a Roman of illustrious family, the Caeonii. Many patrician Roman families in Augustine's era were

becoming Christians. In this they were often led by their
women, who for centuries had been quicker than their men
to discard paganism and become Christians. The Caeonii
had two especially redoubtable women—the older and the
younger Melanias—who zealously worked for the conversion
of the males in the family. So, when Volusian in 411–12 was
dispatched to Africa to be proconsul, the elder Melania wrote
to her Christian contacts in Carthage to get them to befriend
him. One of these, the tribune Marcellinus, saw Volusian
daily; so also did other Christian aristocrats. Volusian was
interested in religion, so conversations on Christianity and
paganism happened easily. When Volusian confronted the
Carthage Christians with questions bigger than they could
cope with, they wrote to Augustine in Hippo for help. So also,
at their urging, did Volusian himself, asking for advice about
"some doubtful points." "I enroll myself with eagerness in
your school," he wrote (Augustine, *Ep* 135). Augustine
responded respectfully and at length to Volusian, whom he
addressed as "noble lord, justly distinguished and excellent
son," adding that Bishop Possidius joined him in sending greet-
ings. To Marcellinus, Augustine responded even more lengthily
and candidly about Volusian's concerns (*Epp* 137–38).

From Volusian—supplemented by Marcellinus—comes a
clear picture of an aristocrat's hesitations. Volusian was
"entangled in doubt" about some of Christianity's primary
beliefs. The incarnation seemed illogical to him: how was it
possible that "the Lord and Ruler of the world filled the
womb of a chaste virgin?" And how could God get involved
in the affairs of individual people, driving out evil spirits, cur-
ing the sick; "these are small things for a god to do."
Marcellinus elaborated on these concerns and added another: the "preaching and doctrine [of Christ] were not adapt-
able to the customs of the state." The teachings of Christ—
for example, that his followers should not return evil for evil,
or give up their cloak when someone took their coat—were
"contrary to the laws of the state." Great evils, Volusian was
convinced, would befall a state that had rulers who observed
teachings such as these, and no aristocrat could espouse
them (*Epp* 135–36).

Augustine dictated replies that took Volusian's queries seriously. Carefully and elegantly he responded to Volusian's doctrinal queries, showing the reasonableness of Christian belief. And these beliefs were being espoused by increasing numbers of people, including (as Volusian certainly knew) aristocrats.

> Though few in number, [the Christians] are spread over the world; with marvelous ease they convert whole peoples; they grow in the midst of enemies; they increase under persecution; and by the pressure of affliction they are scattered to the ends of the earth. Though once the most ignorant, the most lowly, the fewest in number, they become learned, they are ennobled, their numbers are multiplied (*Ep* 137).

Augustine gave Volusian no indication that the aristocrats who had espoused Christianity had been required in any way to change the behavior characteristic of Roman patricians; he had come a long way from Cyprian a century and a half earlier. Nor were the teachings of Jesus that were problematic to Volusian inimical to the interests of the state. They referred not to Christian political morality but to the "interior dispositions of the heart." The behavior of Christian rulers must be governed, not by spineless love but by "a sort of kindly harshness" in the interests of the welfare of others. The good need to wage wars "in order to curb licentious passions by destroying those vices which should have been rooted out and suppressed by the rightful government." If there were hesitations on this, they should be stilled by the advice that John the Baptist gave to soldiers who came to him (Luke 3:14). He had every opportunity to tell them to "throw down their arms and give up military service altogether," but he didn't do so; instead, he told them to avoid undue violence and to be content with their pay. Volusian had heard that Christianity was "opposed to the welfare of the state," but he was misinformed; on the contrary, Christianity was conducive to "the greatest safety of the state." For someone as "distinguished and excellent" as Volusian, conversion would not require a fundamental change in aristocratic behavior (*Epp* 137–38).

### Volusian Joins the Christian Mainstream

Nevertheless, Volusian resisted conversion. Twenty-four years later, in 436, we meet him again, this time in Constantinople where he—still a pagan—had been sent as an ambassador from the Roman court to Constantinople (Gerontius, *Life of Melania* 52–55 tells the story). A marriage of the Western emperor Valentinian III to the Eastern princess Eudoxia had been mooted, and the emperor had called upon Volusian's diplomatic skills to finalize arrangements. As Volusian traveled eastward, another of the Caeonii heard of his mission and herself rushed to Constantinople: where the elder Melania had failed, the younger Melania, now mother of a monastic establishment near Jerusalem, was going to succeed in obtaining the conversion of her uncle.

The aged aristocrat and the wizened nun had an emotional reunion. Volusian was stirred, and no doubt disoriented, by the austere appearance of this now middle-aged noblewoman, who had been so delicately brought up. Melania shifted the topic from her appearance to her appeal to her uncle to convert to Christianity. She has despised the pleasures of the present life, which are fleeting. How about him? "I beg you, approach the bath of immortality, so that you may obtain eternal goods, just as you have enjoyed temporal things." Appealing to her uncle to free himself from demons, she warned him that he would be burned with them in eternal fire if he did not repent. Furthermore, making oblique reference to imperial legislation of 408 and 416 (CT 16.5.42; 16.19.21), she threatened "to take the matter to the emperors."

At this, Volusian was "cut deeply to the heart." He was eager to wash away the "stain" of his misdeeds. But he begged Melania not to "take from me the gift of self-determination" that God had given him. If he should be baptized in response to an imperial command, "I would gain it as through force and would lose the reward of my free decision." This failed to stifle Melania. Through aristocratic contacts she arranged for Bishop Proclus to come to see Volusian. Volusian was deeply impressed by Proclus, through whom he evidently was made a catechumen: "If [in Rome] we had three men there like lord Proclus, no one there would be called a pagan." Some time thereafter, when Volusian's health took a turn for the worse, he was baptized, evidently in bed. Melania had him participate three times in the eucharist, whereupon "she joyfully sent him on in peace to the Lord." Persistence, persuasion, changing social convention, the threat of force, and impending death had finally conquered Volusian. Melania rejoiced; the entire family of the Caeonii was Christian.

A century earlier, in Constantine's baptism, the church had required the emperor to change his lifestyle. But in Volusian's case—from Augustine's correspondence in his early adulthood to Proclus' catechizing and Melania's maneuverings in his last days—there is no hint that conversion required a respectable aristocrat to change. At no point did anyone query his social priorities or invite him to change his behavior in light of Cyprian's criterion—the "example of living in Christ" (*Ad Quirinum* 3.39). In this Volusian's experience was typical. As Rita Lizzi has pointed out, "In order to encourage the conversion of the wealthier citizens, the bishops modulated their preaching, dealing in an appropriate fashion with the topics of wealth and alms-giving" (1990:167). Peter Brown has characterized the result—"a respectable, aristocratic Christianity" (1972:177). And it was now these converted aristocrats who, in collaboration with church leaders, used their kudos and their clout to secure the conversion of their at times uncooperative underlings. Thus the conversion of Europe proceeded.

Wayne Meeks, in his illuminating book *The Origins of Christian Morality*, discusses two types of conversion that he finds in many societies. Through the first kind of conversion, once-respectable citizens become members of groups that deviate from the values of the larger society; their conversion entails "the resocialization into an alternative community." Through the second kind of conversion,

> someone who was leading a dissolute, barren, or otherwise deplorable life... turns about, shapes up, and henceforth exhibits deportment approved by all....

# 7

# Converting the Christians: Caesarius of Arles

## Attracting and Correcting the Pagans

A century after Augustine, Caesarius was bishop of Arles, the leading town of southern Gaul. Caesarius came from a prominent Gallo-Roman family, so his background had prepared him for leadership in Gallic society. His sermons, of which almost 250 have survived, demonstrate that he, like Augustine, had the pastoral and spiritual gifts that were needed to superintend the Christianization of a province. During his long episcopate—Caesarius was bishop from 502 to his death in 542—there were many conversions, which he did much to promote. But it is intriguing to study these conversions, for they show that, as Christianity progressively became the predominant religion of the area, the nature of conversion continued to change.[1]

For the inhabitants of Arles who were outside the church, Caesarius showed missionary concern. He urged his flock:

> You ought to think that every man is your neighbor, even before he is a Christian. For you do not know what kind of a man he will be in the presence of God; you do not know how God has foreknown him.... Our neighbors lie hidden in those men who do not belong to the Church.... [W]e do not know what is going to happen to a man who is either a Jew or a heretic or a

pagan. Perhaps... through the mercy of the Lord he
will be converted to God in such a way that he will
deserve to hold the first place among the saints
(*Sermon* 180.1).

Caesarius was concerned that believers should treat their
non-Christian neighbors well, and also that whenever possible they should be prepared to explain "the mystery of the
Christian religion" to them (*Sermon* 104.6).

But Caesarius was troubled. Pagan rites—as well as conventional Gallic social behavior—obviously appealed to the
people of his diocese. To describe those who resisted their
blandishments, Caesarius drew upon potent words from the
Christian vocabulary: martyrdom and persecution. "All sinners persecute the good, not with sword and stones, but by
their life and morals" (*Sermon* 181.4). Adulterers persecute
the chaste, and whoever bears "witness to Christ for the sake
of justice is without doubt a martyr" (*Sermons* 86.5; 52.1).
This was a matter so serious that Christians must resort to
extreme measures to rip out the roots of seduction.
Especially was this so for the secular rulers: "Formerly the
[princes of the earth] persecuted Christians for the sake of
idols; now they persecute idols for the sake of Christ"
(*Sermon* 142.2). Caesarius especially appealed to landlords
to suppress the paganism of their underlings:

> Chastize those whom you know to be [guilty]; warn
> them very harshly; scold them very severely. And if
> they are not corrected, beat them if you have the
> power; and if they are not improved by this, cut off
> their hair too. And if they still persevere, bind them in
> iron shackles, so that those whom the grace of Christ
> does not hold, a chain may hold (*Sermon* 53.2).

Second-century Christianity, according to Celsus, had
grown not least through the evangelistic activities of marginal people ("bucolic yokels... and stupid women" [Origen,
*Contra Celsum* 3.55]). Four centuries later Caesarius, building on the tradition of Augustine, was now urging it to grow

by top-down means, mobilizing the influence and clout of local elites who were of course mostly male. Caesarius did not see this as persecution. He, anticipating a common reflex of Christendom, reserved the category of persecution for actions that non-Christians committed against Christians.

## Abbreviating the Four Stages

Some people, who responded either to the Christians' pressure or to their neighborliness, continued to approach the church to become catechumens. They did so by well-established means—the four traditional stages of conversion were still functioning in Arles—and thereby they entered into a malleable Stage 2 during which churchmen prepared them for conversion (Beck 1950:166). This was even true of children born to Christian parents. By the early sixth century it was increasingly likely that children of Christian parents would be christened soon after birth; but not always—for some offspring of Christian homes the traditional pattern of adult baptism continued to function. As in Hippo, so in Arles: the catechumens—whether or not they were born into Christian families—were adept at finding excuses to defer their baptism.

Caesarius appealed to them to repent before it was too late: "Do not delay, O man, the remedies of your salvation, because you do not know when your soul may be demanded of you" (*Sermon* 170.4). Although increasingly baptism was taking place at many times in the year, the Easter season remained the church's preferred time for initiation. In the weeks before Easter, Caesarius and other preachers increased the pressure on unbaptized catechumens, urging them to offer their names "several days before Easter" to become *competentes*. If they did so, they received the imposition of hands and the anointing with oil and indicated their readiness for serious, if brief, baptismal preparations. Of course, given the shortness of time—the *Apostolic Tradition's* three years had now been whittled down, via Leo the Great's "Lenten fast," to "ten days or at least a week" in Caesarius's Arles—very little catechism was now possible

(*Sermon* 225.6). But the focus of the baptismal preparations was not pedagogical but spiritual. Caesarius urged his *competentes* to examine their consciences. They were to banish hatred from their hearts, ask forgiveness of those they had harmed, repay anyone they had defrauded, and ask God's mercy if they had committed "theft or murder or adultery" or taken an abortifacient. Thus cleansed, the *competentes*— "kind, humble, mild, and temperate"—could approach the exorcistic scrutinies of the Easter vigil and baptism (*Sermons* 200; 225.6).

## Catechizing in the Midst of Baptismal Revolution

By the early sixth century the *competentes* had come to be of all ages: "All who are baptized are still called infants, whether they are old men or young" (*Sermon* 129.5). A century earlier, in Augustine's time, as in the early Christian centuries, the baptism of Christians was primarily that of consenting adults. At least from the middle of the second century the baptism of infants can be documented, and in some Christian communities this seems to have been relatively widely practiced; but infant baptism, even in North Africa, always remained vastly less common than adult baptism. The church's main mission was to people who were first-generation converts to Christianity, and its baptismal liturgies were designed to incorporate people who chose to adhere to Christ. Not until the eighth century did the church develop liturgies appropriate for those who could not answer for themselves (Whitaker 1970:166; Didier 1965). Insofar as the churches did practice the baptism of young children, it was primarily not of newborn infants but of children who were sickly and in danger of dying (Wright 1987; Wright 1997; Ferguson 1979). As late as the 380s in Antioch, John Chrysostom conceded that he practiced "even the baptism of children" (*Baptismal Instructions* 3.6). At about the same time in Cappadocia, Gregory of Nazianzus preferred to delay baptizing children, if their health permitted, until they were at least three; then they could begin "to listen and to answer," to know the outlines of Christian teaching and to "begin to be responsible for their lives" (*Oratio* 40.18). It was Augustine who really changed things. As David Wright has recently argued, Augustine initiated a "baptismal revolution" that unleashed pastoral and theological forces that fundamentally altered the primitive Christian pattern. Henceforth in the West it would become increasingly difficult not to baptize a newborn immediately; parents became fearful of the spiritual risks of deferring baptism until the paschal season. The ramifications of this transformation—ritual, theological, and pastoral—would profoundly shape the character of Christendom (Wright, forthcoming).

Caesarius found himself in the midst of this baptismal revolution. Some of his baptismal candidates were adults who had sponsors who vouched for their character and joined in the "watching and fasting." Others were children of varying ages whom the heads of their households had brought for baptism. Those who were ill could be baptized immediately, but Caesarius was conservative; he maintained that it was "much better for those who are to be baptized to be kept for the Paschal feast." The children's parents and sponsors "should fast as far as their strength allows, and they should come to vigils rather frequently" (*Sermon* 225.6). In the baptismal rite all the candidates—adults, "little children," and infants—were exorcised. The older candidates renounced Satan and his pomps, and they made a "pact with the Lord" to live a life of continual renunciation and fidelity. For the candidates who couldn't speak for themselves, their parents or sponsors made the pact in their behalf. Then ensued the immersion. "Reborn," the candidates were clad in a "snowy tunic"; spiritually they had crossed the Jordan into the Promised Land. Henceforth they, of whatever age, would "merit to become the house of God" (*Sermons* 12.3; 200.1; 189.2; 115.1).

## The Sponsors' Catechetical Burden

How important the sponsors were in the new scheme of things (Lynch 1986)! Caesarius did not refer to confirmation, which in Gaul had only recently been split off from the

all-embracing baptismal rite of which it had been a part
(Fisher and Yarnold 1992:149). But repeatedly he impressed
upon the sponsors their responsibility before God to catechize their "children."

> Remember the Creed and the Lord's Prayer yourself
> and teach it to your children. I do not know with what
> boldness a man says he is a Christian, if he refuses to
> learn a few lines of the Creed and the Lord's Prayer.
> Remember that you stood surety before God for the
> sons you received in baptism, so always reprove and
> rebuke those whom you adopted at the font just as you
> do those who were born of you.... Do you live in such
> a way that, if your children want to imitate you, they
> will not burn with you in the fire but together with you
> obtain eternal rewards (*Sermon* 13.2; cf. 12.3).

Caesarius warned the sponsors that their charges must
live consistently as Christians. They must take no bribes or
unjust profit; they must not get drunk. Every Sunday they
must go to church, where they must be quiet and not argue
or engage in idle conversation. They must pay their tithes to
the church and "begin to give to the poor." Their entire
behavior must be thoughtful of others: "Above all, do to others what you want to suffer from them." And their lives must
be marked by a constant vigilance against the seductions of
paganism:

> If you still see men fulfilling vows to fountains or trees,
> and... consulting sorcerers, seers or charmers, hang-
> ing devilish phylacteries, magic signs, herbs, or
> charms on themselves or their family, rebuke them
> harshly, telling them that one who does this evil loses
> the sacrament of baptism (*Sermon* 13.2).

So, for the newly baptized converts, what had changed?
Their beliefs had been gradually formed and filled out, and
for some of them even changed. Caesarius's sermons, which
constituted "the catechesis of the church of Arles" (Beck
1950:164), provided a running commentary on the texts of

many biblical books; in these he mingled dogma with morals and narrative. In the prebaptismal sessions, the catechists taught the *competentes* the Creed and the Lord's Prayer. If, by the standards of earlier Christian practice, Caesarius's teaching about belief seems somewhat slender, his teaching about belonging was even more meager. Preaching on Genesis 12, in which Abraham left his kinsfolk and his father's house, Caesarius told his candidates that they would be doing the same: "It is through the gift of Christ's grace... that we can go forth from our country, that is, carnal living, leave our kinsfolk, that is vices and sins, and flee from the home of the devil our father" (*Sermon* 81.2). In the church's early centuries, conversion had led to the forming of a new transnational people, entailing an unprecedented querying of the conventional relationship between religion and national and ethnic identity; now, in Caesarius's Arles as henceforth in Christendom, baptism led to a repudiation of Satan that was somehow consistent with a fusion of Christianity with the candidates' race and place (Wilken 1984:123–24).

Caesarius spent more time talking about behavior than about either belief or belonging, and did so, interestingly, especially when addressing sponsors about the virtues they were to inculcate in their godchildren. The sponsors, after all, had concluded a "pact" with God in behalf of their candidates, and it was their responsibility to "encourage them to good works, not only by words but also by examples" (*Sermons* 229.6; 200.6). So the godchildren were to avoid bad things—consulting fortunetellers, hanging amulets, visiting magicians, being proud and envious. But they were to do good things—eagerly and often attend church, "condemn verbosity,... receive strangers and, in accord with what was done for themselves in baptism, wash the feet of their guests" (*Sermon* 204.3). Caesarius also drummed into people the necessity of tithing and charitable giving: "Above all, give tithes of all your profits to the church for the clergy and the poor; from the nine-tenths which remain in your possession, give alms" (14.3; 1.12).[2]

away from the services (*Sermon* 74.4). Others attended but found ways to demonstrate their disaffection. During services people—"among whom are usually a goodly number of clerics"—engaged in gossip and idle chatter; some talked during the readings, others lay down on the ground (*Sermon* 78.1). A few people came "only to leave"; they bolted the services after the gospel reading—notably before Caesarius's sermons. Caesarius appealed to the people, for the good of their souls, to stay to listen; and just in case, he locked the people in: "he often had the door shut after the reading of the gospel until those who had once been deserters resorted in God's will and at their chastisement and spiritual progress" (*Vita Caesarii* 1.27).

### Converting the Christians— Ratifying the Pact of Baptism

Caesarius repeatedly appealed to the people to observe the pact that they, either personally or through their sponsors, had made with God. They were doing that which they ought not to have done, especially by reverting to pagan worship. Not only did they refuse to destroy pagan shrines; not only did they "rather frequently… make vows to trees, pray to fountains, and practice diabolical augury"; but they also, when someone came to destroy the "diabolical altars," furiously threatened to bludgeon the shrine-destroyers to death. Caesarius found this incomprehensible: "Why, then, did these miserable people come to church? Why did they receive the sacrament of baptism—if afterwards they intended to return to the profanation of idols?" Caesarius warned his people: whoever engages in pagan practice "immediately loses the sacrament of baptism, becoming at once impious and pagan." The only way for such a person to avert eternal punishment was "generous almsgiving together with hard, prolonged penance" (*Sermon* 53.1; 54.1).

To such recidivists, baptized Christians who had "defiled the silk garment of baptism," Caesarius issued a call to conversion (*Sermon* 205.2). "Do not delay to be converted to the Lord, brethren." In sixth-century Arles it was brothers, members of

the Christian family, even members of the clergy, who needed conversion (*Sermon* 2.4). "Be converted," Caesarius
urged them, "and do penance." "Be converted to a better
life" (*Sermons* 108.4; 167.8). They were to remember their
"pact" with the Lord and honor it, turning their backs on
postbaptismal behavior that was loose or pagan. Caesarius
appealed to them regardless of their status in society and the
church; he addressed his call to "both men and women, religious and lay, young and old, boys and girls" (*Sermon* 64.4).
Not only those who committed egregious sins should repent;
so also should those who "do not observe the precepts of
Christ" (*Sermon* 209.3). Caesarius, like Augustine, appealed
to his hearers not to delay: "Now some careless person may
say: When I reach old age, then I shall have recourse to the
healing of repentance." Caesarius was unimpressed. It was
impossible to predict what mischance might come to the
temporizing sinner; but more seriously, genuine repentance
required not only words but generous deeds, and these were
hard to perform on one's deathbed. To urge the unfaithful
faithful to postbaptismal conversion, Caesarius appealed to
the same terrifying text (Sirach 5:8) that a century before
Augustine had used to motivate the catechumens of Hippo to
enroll for baptism: "Do not delay to turn back to the Lord...
for suddenly the wrath of the Lord will come upon you." For
this purpose, Caesarius even adopted an entire sermon of
Augustine:

> You keep adding tomorrow and another tomorrow, but
> neglect to be converted, and do you not fear that sud-
> den death may overtake you? Conversion is a good
> thing. If it is good, let it be done at once (*Sermon* 18.2).

Conversion may have been good; but the difficulty with it, as
Caesarius spelled out its implications, was that it was costly.
Not only did it involve ceasing to do the untoward things that
Caesarius flayed in his sermons. Not only did it involve
beginning to practice the precepts of Jesus. It also involved
acts of reparation and penance. The way to reaffirm the pact
with the Lord came through the now-customary penitential

disciplines of almsgiving, fasting, vigils, and prayers. It also involved the good works of visiting the sick and those in prison, welcoming the strangers, and "recalling the discordant to harmony." And "most of all" this involved "wholehearted love of our enemies" (*Sermons* 60.4; 61.4). Almsgiving was good, but it wasn't enough: "Now if we give alms generously but according to Christ's precepts do not forgive our enemies, we offer our earthly substance to God but subject our soul to the Adversary" (*Sermon* 39.4). When people returned to God in conversion, their submission must be unqualified.

### Conversion—Clerics and Religious

But this, many people objected, was too demanding. And over the years two approaches were emerging that in various ways dealt with this objection. The first was the religious life—monasticism. One of Caesarius's hearers referred to this approach when he blurted out, in response to a call to conversion: "I am young and married, how can I cut my hair or assume the religious habit?" He assumed that the life of conversion that Caesarius had preached was unworldly and could not be realized by people such as himself. Caesarius responded by informing the young man that, married though he was, he could indeed be converted. He could become a disciplined Christian whose behavior was transformed. The point was not to change his clothing but his manner of life. "How can a married man be harmed," Caesarius asked rhetorically, "if he is willing to change his evil habits to good and noble works?" (*Sermon* 56.3).

Conversion, Caesarius believed, was for all Christians. But only for the clergy did it become a requirement. Caesarius stipulated that no layman could be ordained unless at least a year had elapsed since his conversion (4th Council of Arles, c. 2). Shortly after his death, the 5th Council of Orleans (c. 9) stated the same requirement for a bishop; it was essential that they be "instructed more fully, by learned and tested men, in the discipline and spiritual rules" (Gaudemet and Basdevant 1989). At least among the secular Christians, the bishops—like the early Christians—were to be catechized and converted! And yet the connection between the idea of conversion and the monastic life continued to strengthen. Caesarius, in his rules for monks and nuns, himself used the word *converto* to denote becoming a religious, and by the Carolingian era this had become the primary meaning of the word (*Statuta sanctarum virginum* 4, 61; Mohrmann 1961:344).

For the monks and nuns, conversion did not have to do with a change of belief; the religious, as good Catholic Christians, believed the orthodox teaching of the church. But for the religious the term continued to have strong connotations of change in belonging and behavior. For them conversion entailed entry into a religious community that replaced their families as their primary social unit. In this they belonged, lived, and died. The entry into this new life was so momentous and was articulated with vows and ritual of such solemnity that it was often called a "second baptism" (Malone 1951:128). The monks' and nuns' change of behavior was supposed to be correspondingly dramatic, espousing a lifestyle of poverty, chastity, and nonviolence (Cassian, *Conferences* 21.32). As such it carried on into Christendom a witness to the evangelical nonconformity. The fidelity of the religious inspired many people. As Christendom matured in the West, many serious laypeople, who could not aspire to enter the religious life, nevertheless sought to experience something that they called "conversion." Caesarius would have celebrated this—a quality of spirit and life marked by transparency to God and selfless love for God's creatures that set them apart from the "unconverted" (Van Engen 1986:547). The church's leaders could have followed Caesarius in seeking to generalize such conversion for all believers, but this would have drastically restricted the church's capacity to grow and to become the unifying religious institution of a civilization. So they left the attempt to achieve "the perfection of evangelical teaching" (Cassian, *Conferences* 21.33) to monks and nuns, many of whom were faithful to their calling.

### A Community Religion Designed by the People

The second approach, syncretism, on the other hand, was consistent with growth. When Caesarius attempted to get his people—especially in the countryside—to choose between Christianity and paganism, he encountered opposition. When Christians were perplexed about the future or suffered from snakebite, they were likely to go to seers or magicians for help. Caesarius railed at them for "tepid faith" and urged them to be "faithfully converted to God." But he noted that when people recovered after receiving "impious remedies," people were tempted the "more readily to believe in the devil" (*Sermon* 54.3–4). Alas, at times spells and folk remedies seemed to work, and no amount of episcopal harassment would dissuade people from resorting to them.

All over Europe, as Christianity spread northward, people negotiated their own accommodations between the traditional beliefs and practices of the countryside and the new faith that built churches in the towns. An Arian Visigoth named Agilan gave expression to this:

> It is a proverbial saying with us that no harm is done when a man whose affairs take him past the altars of the Gentiles and the Church of God pays respect to both (Gregory of Tours, *History of the Franks* 5.43).

Shortly thereafter Agilan was forcibly converted to Catholicism (Thompson 1960:10–11). But where force was impossible—which was much of the time—the locals were able to extract a bargain from the churchmen. A century after Caesarius, the missionary bishop Eligius was preaching in a village near Noyon, where most people were pagan. When he denounced "diabolical games" and "other superstitions," a local man interrupted him:

> Roman that you are, although you are always bothering us, you will never uproot our customs, but we will go on with our rites as we always have done, and we will go on doing so always and forever. There will never exist the man who will be able to stop us holding our

> time-honored and most dear games (Fouracre
> 1979:82).

These people would hold their games; they also would be
Christians. The people's choice was not whether they would
be Christians or pagans; in a milieu of compulsion, that
choice was not given to them. Rather, it was what sort of
Christians they would be. For most people the solution was
"a community religion they designed for themselves"
(Klingshirn 1994:243).

How do we evaluate this community religion?
Missiologists have in recent years begun to think seriously
about inculturation, and historians have begun to learn from
them.[3] When the Christian message is inserted into a cultural framework, if the messengers are insensitive to the local
culture the result can be cultural imperialism. On the other
hand, if they grant too much hegemony to the local culture,
the result at best is "syncretism" and at worst "Christopaganism" (Chupungco 1989:29; Tippett et al. 1975). Things
are most wholesome when sensitive interchange takes place
leading to "a truly critical symbiosis." But for this to happen,
there must be a second stage—a time of "pastoral follow-up
work," of catechizing and life formation enabling the new
faith to express its genius in the institutions and reflexes of
its new host culture (Kahl 1978:49). In early medieval
Europe, such a second stage did not materialize. The records
of church leaders show their preoccupations: they were concerned about property disputes and episcopal jurisdictions,
not about catechism (Stancliffe 1979:59). For the children
who were baptized as infants, despite Caesarius's injunctions
to the sponsors, the sources contain virtually no record of
formal instruction. Eventually, in Carolingian times, a concern for catechism becomes evident in the sources; but by
the standards of Cyprian or Chrysostom or even Caesarius,
it is rudimentary. The catechetical documents that emerge—
such as that of Pirmin—were largely based on Augustine's
*First Catechetical Instruction* (Belche 1977; Engelmann

1959). But, as we have observed, Augustine had not intended this to be a catechism; rather, he designed it to be a promotional taster for those whom the catechists were trying to persuade to receive catechism. Most early-medieval churchmen, lacking even these catechetical materials, were content if the people learned the Lord's Prayer and the Creed (Jegen 1967:209).

As Europeans were converted and Europe became Christendom, the host cultures exercised a tremendous power over the emerging religion of the West.

# 8

# Christendom—Product of Conversion—and Some Clues About the Future of Christianity

Let us now briefly examine the "Christian civilization" that was the product of the conversion that we have been studying. In medieval Latin, this civilization was called *Christianitas*; in the Anglo-Saxon world, since the ninth century it has been called "Christendom" (Van Engen 1986:540–41). The word has been widely used but rarely defined, but in the title of Peter Brown's recent book, *The Rise of Western Christendom: Triumph and Diversity,* A.D. *200–1000,* there are hints of a definition.[1] Because Brown begins his study of Christendom's rise in 200, the term *Christendom* is evidently not identical with Christianity, whose roots go further back; because he ends his study in the year 1000, Christendom had evidently risen by then. It had not only risen but had taken hold of the minds and reflexes of Western people in a way that seemed unshakable. As Brown noted, "Christendom was a notion that now carried the charge of perpetuity" (Brown 1996:315). So what was this notion, and the reality that underlay it, that was the basis for the Christian civilization of the West?

## The Conversion of Clovis

Two more conversion stories, each indicating a turning point in the Christianization of the West, will help us sense the salient characteristics of Christendom. The first story is that of Clovis, king of the Franks.[2] In the late fifth century, despite the intercessions and articulate witness of his queen Clotild, Clovis remained resistant to her Christian faith. But in 496, when his troops were being slaughtered by the Alamanni, Clovis prayed for help to Jesus Christ. "I want to believe in you," he prayed, "but I must first be saved from my enemies." Whereupon the Alamanni turned tail and submitted to Clovis. Remigius, bishop of Rheims, at the request of Clotild came to Clovis to "impart the word of salvation" to him, urging him to forsake his idols and to believe in the true God. When Clovis learned that his troops would follow him in converting to Christianity, Clovis applied for baptism. We do not know how long his baptismal preparations lasted or what his catechesis consisted of. What does one teach a Frankish king about belief, belonging, and behavior? But we do know, from Bishop Avitus of Vienne, that Clovis was made a *competens*. When Christmas Eve came—it was evidently decided not to make the King wait until Easter—Clovis entered the baptistery in Rheims, which incense had transformed into a "perfumed paradise." There he was initiated.

> When a crowd of bishops around you, in the ardor of their holy ministry, poured over your royal limbs the waters of life; when that head feared by the peoples bowed down before the servants of God; when your royal locks, hidden under a helmet, were steeped in holy oil; when your breast, relieved of its cuirass, shone with the same whiteness as your baptismal robes.

This account indicates elements of continuity with Christian tradition: the immersion (if not submersion) in running water; the anointings with oil; the white baptismal robes. It also indicates some rather arresting shifts. In a gesture toward the nakedness of earlier baptismal practice, the king divested himself of his armor, but he continued, even in the baptismal pool, to wear his helmet![3] Bishop Avitus' assurance to the king was also novel: "Do not doubt... that this soft clothing will give more force to your arms: whatever Fortune has given up to now, this Sanctity will bestow."

Three thousand of Clovis' troops were baptized at the same time, presaging the collective tribal baptisms that occurred as Christianity conquered Western Europe. In the ensuing years before his death in 511, Clovis proceeded to solidify his control over large areas of Gaul, in the course of which he killed off every relative that he could find (*History of the Franks* 2.42). Clovis was not interested in rivals.

Was Clovis converted? Well, that depends. As John Moorhead has noted, "Murderous behavior does not disprove the reality of religious convictions." By the standards of the late fifth century, Clovis was now a Christian, and he encouraged the spread of Christianity among the Merovingian Franks. Indeed, for the Franks "conversion was a *rite de passage...* on the way to becoming civilized" (Moorhead 1985:338–39). But by earlier standards, had Clovis become a Christian? For Bishop Cyprian there would not have been, as there clearly was for Bishop Avitus, a neat equation between aristocratic ideals and Christianity. Nor would there have been—even in the case of Clovis's hero, Constantine—a sense that a monarch could be converted without making fundamental changes in his behavior (Russell 1994:150–53). Nevertheless, Clovis's conversion was of highest importance in Christianity's conquest of the West. In content, it was the religious equivalent of "fast-food": unlike the conversion of earlier centuries, its ingredients—repudiating idol worship and submitting to the clergy ("[bowing] down before the servants of God")—could be produced quickly. As such it was a template for the conversion of Clovis's troops and then of innumerable Europeans, and it both reflected and shaped the vision and values that would be characteristic of Christendom in the West. In religio-geopolitics it was also important: it marked the turning point as Western Christianity's heartland moved from the Mediterranean to Northern Europe.

### The Conversion of the Jews of Clermont

Our second story comes from Clermont, in what is today south-central France.[4] For centuries the Christian and pagan populace of Clermont had coexisted with a large number of Jewish neighbors. Every year in the Easter season, the bishop of Clermont, another Avitus, prayed for the conversion of the Jews. On Good Friday in 576 his prayers were answered, in part—a Jew asked to be baptized. The sources do not tell us whether he was catechized on Holy Saturday (how much, we might wonder, could he be taught in one day?); but they do report that on Easter, as he was processing through the streets in his white robes with other newly baptized people, a Jew poured rancid oil on his head—a bitter parody of the anointing that he had just received. This led to weeks of intracommunal tension in which Avitus with difficulty restrained the Christian populace of Clermont from taking violent direct action against their Jewish neighbors. Finally, on Ascension Day, a Christian mob broke loose from a procession that Avitus was leading and razed the synagogue to the ground. Avitus responded to this arson attack with severe words, not to the mob but to the Jews:

> I do not use force nor do I compel you to confess the Son of God. I merely preach to you.... If you are prepared to believe what I believe, then become one flock, with me as your shepherd. If not, then leave this place.

As the Jewish leaders pondered this ultimatum, a crowd of Christians assisted them in their deliberations by besieging the house where they were meeting. Most Jews agreed to be converted, and on Pentecost more than five hundred were washed with water, anointed with chrism, and, white-robed, were "brought... together into the bosom of the Mother Church." There was great joy in Clermont, for now everyone there was a Christian.

Everyone? Yes. The members of the Jewish community who resisted conversion left Clermont and moved to Marseilles where their existence, though no doubt uncomfortable, would be tolerated.

This account, like that of Clovis's conversion, has elements that are in keeping with Christian tradition. Baptism at Easter and Pentecost, the immersions and anointings, the white robes of the neophytes—all these are familiar. And yet something is new. Conversion, which had made Christians into distinctive people—resident aliens—now was something that made people ordinary, not resident aliens but simply residents. So Bishop Avitus, in enforcing the religious uniformity of his city, was innovating. By bringing into being a city in which there would be no non-Christian options, he was an architect of Christendom.

Of course, there were innumerable conversions during these years, as Christianity became the religion of Western Europe and Christendom took its characteristic shape. Many of these were undramatic—serfs responding to the importunity of their lords—or group events, as in the conversion of Clovis's troops. But for many others there was no longer need of conversion. The contours of Christian experience had shifted. Whereas up to the time of Augustine there had been four stages of initiation and incorporation into the church, there were now typically two. The first stage was brief and obligatory—baptism in the days or months after birth. The second stage would happen later and would take longer—if it took place at all—when confirmation happened and when parents instructed their children and godparents instructed their godchildren in the beliefs and behavior of the Christian church. Indeed, at this time of the rapid spread of Christianity into new territories, it was vitally necessary that the baptizands be taught well. The heroic and valorous values of the folk, the glorious narratives of warriors, the adulation of wealth and strength—all of these were as firmly in place in seventh-century Gaul as the pagan values and narratives had been in third-century Rome. If Christianity were to be a religion of revelation that could challenge the commonplaces of Gallic society, if new habits were to be taught and new role models were to be adopted, there would have to be some form of postbaptismal pastoral follow-up (Kahl 1978:49).

Instead, it appears that at times the church leaders were not interested in newness. For example, the bishops did not tell Clovis, as their predecessors had told Constantine, that he would need to be catechized to become a Christian. Still less did they tell him that he would need to change his priorities and behavior—even that to be baptized he would have to take off his helmet. Instead, Bishop Avitus promised Clovis that the Christian God would "give more force to your arms" (Hillgarth 1986:77). Conversion would make Clovis—as well, no doubt, as his three thousand comrades in arms—even more effective in doing what they already excelled at. So Clovis and his troops would be normal Gauls who somehow were also Christians. To be sure, there would be, as there always is and as there had been from Christianity's beginnings, a *conversion continuée*, a reciprocal accommodation of Christianity with its host culture (Fontaine 1972:580). But how were the balances tipped? The pre-Constantinian Christians had borrowed from the story and iconography of Orpheus to express their commitment to Christ as the Good Shepherd. In Clovis's Gaul, Christians drew upon Germanic ideas of *Heil* to ratify an emperor's war making. Both represent an interplay of Christianity and culture, but are they qualitatively different? Is the thesis of this book correct—that there was indeed a change of conversion? And what should we call the result? According to the traditional view, the conversion of Clovis was the culmination of the Christianization of Europe; according to Roman Catholic historian James C. Russell, it was symbolic of the "Germanization of Christianity" (Russell 1994). However we evaluate the evidence, the result of the conversions was the civilization known as "Christendom."

## Characteristics of Christendom

What then were the characteristics of Christendom? In the time of Charlemagne, things were of course very different from the way they were in the times of Calvin or the young Karol Woytila: there have been many varieties of Christendom. But there have been, I believe, common traits, assumptions, and values that, over a period of more than a millennium, keep recurring. These are sufficiently similar to justify a shared category called "Christendom"—a culture seeking to subject all areas of human experience to the

Lordship of Christ. Its institutions and mindsets are still with us in the West.[5] And I believe that these characteristics relate directly to the manner in which the leaders and many of their people came to view the three areas of conversion—belief, belonging, and behavior. Let us look at these in turn.

### A Common Belief: Orthodox Christianity

The belief system of Christendom is that of orthodox Christianity as affirmed by the religious and civil leaders. This provides "the structural ideology" of the entire society. Christianity suffuses the "secular"; it shapes society's politics, institutions, values, and terms of reference (Ellul 1986:39). Regardless of whether people flout its norms or gossip in church services, Christianity provides the religious symbolism, rituals, and "noise" that give to the civilization its characteristic ambiance—and no doubt to many people their faith and inner security (MacMullen 1984:83).

*Heresy is not tolerated:* The state, at the behest of the church, in the late fourth century moved to outlaw heresy even before it banned rival religions. In Christendom it is supremely important that people think the right things about God. Orthodox Christianity will allow no rivals, for truth and unity are important. Religiously, a Christendom society is a one-party state. Its thinkers may debate many issues, but they cannot query the church's credal documents or challenge its society-embracing ecclesiology. In this sense, "heresy" (from the Greek *hairesis*, a school of thought based on choice) is never to be tolerated. In Christendom, error has no rights. The only other religion that may be tolerated in some places—for example, in sixth-century Marseilles though not in Avitus's Clermont—is Judaism.

*Unofficial alternatives live on:* In Christendom there are, as we have seen, many pre-Christian local beliefs and practices that survive. Some of these, as people are converted, have been quietly Christianized. But others have been vigorously opposed by leaders such as the sixth-century bishop,

Martin of Braga, who appealed to Galician Christians to "consider the nature of the pact which you made with God in baptism," or which others "promised for you" (*On the Castigation of Rustics* 16, Hillgarth 1986:62). These foolish Galicians had solemnly renounced the devil, but then had gone on practicing such devilish ceremonies as "lighting candles besides stones and trees and springs, or where three roads meet," muttering pagan incantations, and wearing charms. Despite official opposition, many of these practices have proved immensely durable in Christendom, and many leaders have been less opposed than Martin to "dual faith practices" (Jones and Pennick 1995:134).

*Religious instruction is often rudimentary:* In Christendom catechesis takes place in two ways: as a second stage in a two-stage initiatory process (the first stage being the baptismal rites); or as the informal modeling and instruction provided by parents and godparents. In both ways it varies considerably from situation to situation; but the catechesis is often rudimentary, for there are no religious alternatives to challenge and clarify the thinking of ordinary people. Furthermore, from the time of Caesarius onward there has been a general assumption that the convictions of Christendom are obvious; people who live in a Christendom society know what its beliefs and practices are. Churchmen have often viewed catechesis in either of its forms as successful if it has imparted knowledge of the Lord's Prayer, the Apostles' Creed, and possibly the Decalogue (e.g., Hillgarth 1986:161).

*The society's symbols, art, and ritual are Christian:* Christian themes pervade the Christendom society; they provide a rich fund of narratives and images for the artists and form the consciousness of the people at every turn. To some people, who are not persuaded by the dominant beliefs, this can feel oppressive. But the Christian society's iconography is enlarged by borrowing images from the natural world, astrology, and non-Christian mythology.

### A Common Belonging

In Christendom the members of civil society and members of the Christian church coincide precisely. John Van Engen has observed that "after about the year 1000, Christendom... included every person in medieval Europe except the Jews" (1986:1046). In Christendom everyone is a Christian. And every Christian is not a resident alien (*paroikos*) but a resident, a *parochianus*, an inhabitant of a "parish" that as a geographical entity is equally useful for religious and civil purposes; its inhabitants are all "parishioners." The result is a homogeneous Christian society. People are Christians, not because of what they believe (which may wander wildly) nor because of how they behave (which may resemble the ancient Teutons more than the early Christians), but rather because they belong—and their belonging is rooted in the primal realities of genes and geography. At times, as in sixth-century Marseilles, Jewish people are a tolerated exception; at other times they are exploited or persecuted.

*Recruitment—the christening of all infants:* In the early years, as Christianity spreads, initiation will be by the baptism of people who undergo, generally as adults, some form of conversion of their beliefs, behavior, and belonging, often accompanied by a potent experience of God. As the values of Christendom spread, baptism is increasingly of infants soon after their birth, whom preachers may later remind of the promises that sponsors made in their behalf. In many societies in the Christendom centuries, it has been illegal to deprive infants of baptism. Baptismal services, which for the pre-Christendom Christians had been significant liminal events, became routinized; because they were unavoidable, they became ritually perfunctory (Khatchatrian 1982).

*The church and its constituent parishes are large:* Because everyone is a Christian, the church is numerically all-encompassing, and local congregations often become very large. Attendance at worship services may however be erratic, and behavior at them may be inattentive or irreverent.

*Church/state symbiosis:* In Christendom there is a mutually reinforcing relationship between church and state. *Regnum* and *sacerdotium* are in a symbiotic relationship. The church provides the state with reliable religious legitimation; liturgically its services express the unity of the civic body. The state in turn provides the church with protection and resources; it defends the church's monopoly and its place in the symbolic center of society. If necessary, the state may also provide assistance in settling ecclesiastical disputes or in doing messy things such as executing heretics, who (in the language of sixteenth-century England) will be "delated to the secular arm."

*Lack of choice:* For the people of Christendom, there is no choice (Herrin 1987:479). They must belong to the Christian community, which local power-holders view as "orthodox." This society-encompassing community comes into existence through the use of a variety of sanctions, from neighborly suasion through the application of police powers; and it exists as these operate on a day-to-day basis. Often there are laws that require church attendance and financial support of the churches (tithes and other church taxes), but generally there is a good deal of leeway for various forms of laxity and nonobservance. But this must not represent another belief system or religious authority, for that would threaten the unitary nature of the Christendom society.

*Church and world:* In Christendom societies, the New Testament concept of "world" is spiritualized (as in Augustine's *civitas terrena*) or projected outward onto non-Christendom societies.

*Clericalism:* Within Christendom the fundamental division is not between church and world but between *clergy* and *laity*. A professionalized caste of Christians, with its own hierarchical gradations, is separated from other Christians by various forms of ordination and induction, liminal events that are as imposing ritually as baptism has come to be unimposing.

The clergy serves the populace by providing religious leadership and other services.

*Localism:* In Christendom, in which everyone is Christian, there is a strong identification between belonging to the church and other sources of identity—genes and geography. Christendom Christians may be aware that they are part of a universal, catholic church, and some of them may speak a universal Christian language (Latin in the West); but local solidarities are much more potent than transnational ones, as becomes evident when Christian states go to war against each other.

*Mission:* In Christendom societies, mission often receives little emphasis, for the churches concentrate upon the pastoral care of their people and the maintenance of their structures. When missionary concern arises, "missions" may result; but they often take place outside the geographical territory of the Christendom church, to foreigners. At home, Christendom leaders may see the need of missionizing their own people. But often, when this happens, the language that is used is one that connotes a restoration of something that has become impaired or fallen asleep—"renewal" or "revival" or "reevangelization."

### A Common Behavior

*Behaving "like a Christian":* In Christendom, Christian behavior is rooted in common sense, custom, and Scripture, especially the Old Testament (the Ten Commandments may be emphasized). Unlike the early centuries, in which extended catechism study prepared converts to live Jesus' teachings, in Christendom, Christian behavior has come to reflect the common sense of the host societies. It has come to be normal, in many senses of that term; it is not odd and does not challenge conventional "Christian" wisdom.

*Enforcement of behavioral norms:* This is accomplished by the pressure of neighbors; by the church, whose preachers may remind people of the "pact" that they concluded with God in baptism; and by legislation of the state. The Christendom state seeks to legislate Christian morals for society, with appropriate penalties for infraction. Civil courts, reinforced at times by church courts, may enforce these laws.

***Exceptionally committed Christians:*** In most Christendom societies there are people whose religious commitments are especially intense. It is these people who are likely to have had a life-changing experience, which they may call "conversion." Through this experience they are at times drawn to forms of religious expression and to choices about life priorities that may strike others as being "enthusiastic." A recurring theme among such Christians is a desire to find ways to practice and embody Christ's Sermon on the Mount teachings, which some Christendom traditions have called "counsels of perfection." These people are often counseled to become members of the clergy or of religious communities whose rituals of adherence, with their imposingly liminal quality, have at times been called a "second baptism." Christendom cultures honor committed minorities, provided they do not suggest that their way of life ought to constitute the way of life for "normal" Christians.

### Coercion

This underlies all three characteristics of Christendom. Scholars have found differing ways to describe coercion's varied forms. Sir Herbert Butterfield, as we have noted, wrote of inducement and compulsion; more colloquially, Michele Renee Salzman spoke of "the carrot and the stick," while Ramsay MacMullen referred with typical flair to "flattery and battery."[6] Christendom's uniform belief, its homogeneous belonging, and its common behavior in significant measure spread because they were made into an offer that people couldn't refuse. People learned: things go better for you if you're a Christian—an "orthodox" Christian, that is. Neighborly suasion was potent, but where this didn't work (and neighbors were at times remarkably indulgent of their nonconforming friends), it was reinforced by the powers of the civil authorities. There was also financial coercion. Beginning with the second council of Mâcon in 585 (canon 5), the church in the West required all Christians to pay a tax of 10 percent of their incomes—called the *tithe*—for the support of the church's institutions and leaders (Gaudemet and Basdevant 1989:2.462). In some societies, governments required people to attend church services, although they often allowed a good deal of leeway for laxity and nonobservance. Participation in public institutions—government, the universities, the law courts—was commonly restricted to members of the orthodox church. In schools and prisons, attendance at chapel services was obligatory. And for those who didn't fit, the consequences could be dire. Christendom Christians never called any of this persecution: in the lexicon of Christendom, persecution is what non-Christians do to Christians.

### Living in the Shadow of Christendom

So in Christendom, the incentives to being a Christian have been imposing. What happens without these incentives? What has happened when measures of inducement and compulsion, initially applied in the fourth century, are peeled away? In many Western societies the peeling away has been gradual, taking place layer by layer over many centuries, in revulsion at bloody religious wars between Christian powers, and under pressure from both the Enlightenment and Christian nonconformist bodies. But in many places elements of Christendom survive. Examples of this in England are at times institutional—for example, the twenty-six Anglican bishops who sit by right of office in the House of Lords; they are also nostalgic—for example, the "Keep Sunday Special" campaign, which has sought by law to preserve a special status for the Christian holy day.

Nevertheless, throughout most of the West, Christendom is in a state of decrepitude if not decomposition. In many countries shoppers flood the malls on Sundays, while Sunday morning has become a special time for sporting events. And people vote with their feet. In most Western societies, polls show that a majority of people believe in some sort of God, but church attendance has become a countercultural activity. It is strongest in the United States, where there has been no established church and where competition between religious groups has been intense. Church attendance is weakest in countries such as those of Scandinavia, where totalistic churches (without vigorous nonconformist competitors) continue to have pretensions of universality.

Wherever we live in the West, we will go on living in the shadow of Christendom. The setting for God's mission in the West will be post-Christendom, and the legacy of Christendom will affect our life and witness in many ways. Theologians will continue to debate the history and present applicability of Christendom models (Hauerwas and Willimon 1989; O'Donovan 1996; Bolt and Muller 1996). I believe that the experience of the West indicates that a unitary Christian society cannot be built without compulsion. And compulsion, as a result of our Christendom past, is impossible in post-Christendom. We've been there, done that, and cannot do it again.

But, as we live in Christendom's shadow, the effects of Christendom upon the future of Christianity in the West will be multivalent and ambiguous. The sheer immensity of achievement of Christian artists and intellectuals throughout the Christendom centuries exercises a well-merited appeal upon the minds and sensibilities of many people today. A sample of this is a recent CD of Frank Martin's *Mass for Double Choir*. In the 1920s Martin, a devout Reformed composer from Switzerland, set to music the quintessential liturgical text of the West. In the late 1990s the choir of Westminster Cathedral in London recorded it. This is music of ethereal beauty, performed with searing intensity; for good reason it won *Gramophone* magazine's Record of the Year award for 1998 (Hyperion CDA 67017). This ecumenical product of Christendom has enriched my life. I can imagine it enriching the lives of thousands of Westerners, conveying in a de-spirited culture the joy and wonder of the numinous and possibly drawing some of them, to their astonishment, toward a living faith in God. But there are other relics of Christendom that are ugly and unworthy, and for many people these will be an impediment to coming to faith. Among these, in my view, are approaches and institutions that subject people to the control of Christians. Especially as the millennium approaches, many Western Christians have succumbed to a nostalgic prescription for the future in which God, working through *re*vival or *re*newal or *re*evangelization will once again bring about a world that Christians can rule. It is likely that many Westerners will resist this, as they resist Christianity in general, because they associate it with things that authority figures have forced them to say or do. Because of Christendom, when Christianity is mentioned they will experience boredom or revulsion.

### Relevant Old Ideas for Christianity's Future

So we are living in post-Christendom. But this is not a reason to despair. We can instead view it as liberation in which weighty impedimenta have been lifted from the shoulders of Christians. A post-Christendom era this may be, but it by no means is a post-Christian era. In the West as well as globally, the church of Jesus Christ is living, vibrant, and full of hope and new ideas; in many parts of the world it is growing rapidly. As Herbert Butterfield sensed fifty years ago, this is "the most important and the most exhilarating period in the history of Christianity for fifteen hundred years" (1949:135). And it is striking that many of the new ideas of Christians today are in fact *old* ideas. The early church is of course far from us, and many of its practices are marked by what seems to us to be a "disturbing strangeness" (Brown 1989:xv). Nevertheless, in the past forty years liturgical scholars, pastoral theologians, and missiologists have all found insights in the early church that have transformed the worship and practice of countless contemporary Christians (see, e.g., Field 1997). As Butterfield predicted, the early church has already been a source of "relevant clues" for Christians in post-Christendom. It can, I believe, be a source for many more.

## Missiological Alertness

In conclusion, I will mention three clues that I find relevant to the Christian mission to Western culture at the turn of the millennium. The first of these has to do with missiological alertness. The early Christians were alert to the dominant cultural patterns of their civilization. They faced the task of inculturating their message in societies whose narratives and folkways they needed to evaluate; some they used, some they adapted, some they rejected. So they were able to draw upon the narratives and images of their time while working in their communities for a deep appropriation of a counternarrative of a God whose perfect self-disclosure is Jesus Christ; of a God of whom it could be said, "Coercion is not God's way of working" (*Ep to Diognetus* 7.4). Thinking missiologically, they asked in case after case whether a given practice was life-giving or whether it led to bondage.

Regarding bondage and addiction, early Christian thinkers and catechists were particularly sensitive to the way that conventional folkways—doing what everybody did—trapped people in deathly, demon-beset cages. Justin was aware of the way that people in Rome, in their addiction to occult practices, to sexual adventure, to ever-increasing wealth and property, to hating and killing people of different tribes, were the demons' "slaves and servants" (1 *Apol* 14). Cyprian knew that he—always expecting to wear and eat the best—had been trapped in "gilded torments" (*Ad Donatum* 12). At the time of his conversion, as throughout his life as a Christian, Augustine was hyper-aware of the imprisoning "chain of sexual desire" (*Confessions* 6.13). And Chrysostom saw the oath—not just false swearing (perjury) but even truthful swearing—as a "destructive drug" (*Baptismal Instr* 10.18). These were missiological insights, for they pointed to areas in which the good news of Jesus could set people free. And at least some of the catecheses of early Christianity were aimed at forming communities of free people in which the addictions that blighted pagan society were being addressed and overcome.

A comparable missiological thinking is necessary in the contemporary West. Imagining that in our postmodern era there are no metanarratives, we tend not to look beneath the surface. One person who does is Walter Brueggemann, who with unusual breadth of vision indwells the biblical narrative. As a result, he proposes "military consumerism" as a dominant narrative of our time (Brueggemann 1997:718). Is he right? What other metanarratives can we detect? What aspects of our contemporary cultures can Christians affirm with delight as signs that the Spirit of Jesus is at work in the world? Which of the legacies of Christendom are helpful? Which are distracting and counterproductive? What are the addictions of our time? Justin would not have much difficulty seeing that sexual expression has addictive power in Western society. In places he would also find people whose lives have been captivated by occult practice. Would Justin discern that today, as in second-century Rome, wealth and violence have as much addictive power as either sex and the occult? If we shared the breadth of Justin's perspectives, we might be able to announce with new winsomeness and grace the message of Jesus Christ, who sets people free and gives them life in all its abundance. Preaching could take on a new pastoral relevance; and catechism could deal with practical ways to free people from the full range of addictions that they face.

## Conversion that Changes Behavior
## as well as Belief and Experience

A second relevant clue has to do with the ingredients of conversion. We have noted that pre-Christendom conversion involved comprehensive change in the candidates' belief, belonging, and behavior—and that this might be accompanied by a powerful experience. In the fourth and fifth centuries, the balance began to shift: teaching came to give preponderant attention to correct belief, whereas instruction about behavior atrophied (Kreider 1996; Ferguson, forthcoming). In the late fourth century another powerful engine that changed conversion took place—the conversion of Augustine

of Hippo, who described this powerfully and with psychological profundity in his *Confessions*. Augustine's *Confessions*
had a delayed effect on the churches' understanding of conversion; we have watched him in Hippo continuing to use the
catechetical and ritual practices of earlier centuries, as did
Caesarius a century later in Arles. Nevertheless, later
Christians—especially in the Protestant traditions—have
taken experience to be the most important component of
conversion. That is why historians can talk about
Constantine's visionary experience of 312 as his conversion.
That also is why contemporary evangelistic courses often
place heaviest emphasis upon correct belief leading to over-
powering experience.

The early Christians lead us to reconsider the balance of
ingredients in conversion. They wrote relatively little about
experience; there is no extensive literature of interiority before
Augustine. They did of course emphasize right belief; already
in Justin and Irenaeus this is very evident. But the emphasis in
the early Christian liturgies of a radical shift in the believers'
sense of belonging—their affinity and allegiance—seems
extreme to us. Even stranger to us is the *Apostolic Tradition*'s
focus upon transformed behavior as the heart of catechism.
This strikes us as genuinely bizarre. How could a
Christianity that appears so "legalistic" flourish?

But we might well ask ourselves: Do the early Christians
have anything to say to us? Was it helpful to posit that
insight into truth comes out of practical engagement, that
learning is a product of action? If so, might this be the reason that early Christian conversions produced people whose
approach to the addictions of their time was transformed,
whereas programs of evangelistic teaching in our time leave
people "converted" but unchanged?

### The Power of the Catechetical Process

A third relevant clue has to do with the formative power of
the catechetical process. The *Apostolic Tradition* and other
early documents assume that it took years of formation
before one was ready to become a Christian, and these were

years in which powerful things happened. The commitment
of sponsors to attend catechetical sessions with the candidates dramatized the new affinities—and the new community
of solidarity and support—that would come through conversion.
The teaching and example of the catechists and sponsors and
the practical involvement of the catechumens concentrated
on transforming the catechumens' behavior in ways conso-
nant with the church's understanding of truth. The candidates seem to have learned about Christianity by observing
the Christians in action and by doing what they did; we read
that as a catechumen Cyprian "loved the poor" (*Vita
Cypriani* 6). And the catechists' question must have been:
Has Cyprian, and have the other catechumens, made
progress in dealing with the addictions in their lives? So the
catechetical process was designed to impart freedom in
Christ, and carefully considered rituals marked the stages in
the catechumen's journey.

What relevance does this have for us at the end of the
second millennium? One of the exciting aspects of being a
Christian today is to observe a rediscovery of the importance
of significant prebaptismal formation. Theologians in many
Christian traditions have participated in this rediscovery
(Hauerwas 1991; Westerhoff 1992; Abraham 1989). But no
church has done more to develop and propagate these
insights than the Roman Catholic Church with its Rite for
the Christian Initiation of Adults. The RCIA has had powerful effect not only on Roman Catholicism but also on many
other Christian traditions who have learned from it. I find it
fascinating that this reenergizing of the catechetical process
has been coupled with a rediscovery of early Christian rites
of initiation. Liturgical theologians such as the Lutheran S.
Anita Stauffer have drawn deeply from fourth-century models
(Stauffer 1994). In a growing number of Roman Catholic,
Episcopalian, and Lutheran churches, baptism may take
place by immersion in cruciform baptisteries dug into church
floors. In many free churches baptisms will go on taking
place, as they have for many years, in rivers and tanks. When
people are converted in post-Christendom, the candidates

will be more aware than in Christendom days that they are
dying to old options and rising to new possibilities and
power. For understandable reasons, this new birth, which
involves a life-encompassing transformation, will increasingly be expressed with appropriately drastic ritual.

It may be, as William Harmless comments, that the RCIA
has developed the ritual dimensions of the journey of conversion more than the ethical dimensions (Harmless
1995:20); but his book and the work of a host of catechists
on many continents point out that behavioral change must
be a central component in conversion. The conference of
Catholic bishops in the United States has not long ago asserted
with reference to militarism:

> It is clear today, perhaps more than in previous gen-
> erations, that convinced Christians are a minority in
> nearly every country of the world.... As believers we
> can identify rather easily with the early Church as a
> company of witnesses engaged in a difficult mission.
> To be disciples of Jesus requires that we continually go
> beyond where we now are (*Challenge* 1983:78–79).

To be a creative minority whose members, engaged in a
difficult mission, know how to make peace and to engage
with the other addictions of postmodern society—this
requires catechetical formation that has moral substance as
well as the experience of God's grace, love, and power in
appropriate ritual. The early Christians might ask us: Do you
really want your converts to change? You typically assign
ordinands to take part in practical assignments as a part of
their ordination courses. You assume that it is important for
their formation that they help out in projects such as drop-
in centers for homeless people. Why not make such experiential assignments a part of the catechesis of all baptismal
candidates according to their particular needs for learning?
And as to addiction, could it be that twelve-step groups are
closer to early Christian practice than much that goes on in
churches? One can imagine Justin being at home in a group
whose members say, "I am (Name), and I have taken most

pleasure in increasing my wealth and property" (1 *Apol* 14). Such a moral catechesis, practically and confessionally facing the addictions of our time, might produce churches in which freedom and joy were possible.

### The Relevance of Conversion

Would churches like this grow? Who can tell? Our study of conversion across five early Christian centuries has shown us that for several centuries the church grew because it was addressing people's needs and liberating them from the compulsions that were disfiguring their society. Thereafter conversion changed. In the fourth century and beyond, the church continued to grow more rapidly than ever, but by becoming conventional and compulsory. We can learn from these centuries of experience, engage in diachronological conversation with this experience, and ponder what impact this conversation might have for the concern of our series—Christian Mission and Modern Culture.

It could be that what we are learning from the early Christians could transform the life and mission of our churches. Consider one thing: at the end of the twentieth century the lifestyle of the West, according to meteorologists, is polluting the ecosystem in an unsustainable way; for example, the United States, with less than 5 percent of the world's population, consumes nearly 30 percent of the world's resources and contributes a lion's share of the carbon dioxide pollution (Myers 1997:33–34).[7] Further, the disjunction between rich and poor is relentlessly widening, with effects that pollute the social as well as the ecological environment. And ironically, in the rich West, in the midst of a glut of material, there is a shortage of nonmaterial values. People have no time; in a throwaway culture they do not really cherish material things; there is a crisis of relationships and a heartrending dearth of joy.

What if the theologians and pastors of our time, thinking missiologically in the tradition of the early Christians, pondered our era and proposed means of conversion that addressed its addictions that lead to ecological crisis? What if our churches catechized believers new and old into people who, like Cyprian, "love the poor"? What if they, like Justin, inculcated values, rooted in the teachings of Jesus, of sharing and praying for enemies? What if our churches' initiatory rites—as the globe warms and the ecological crisis intensifies—baptized people into communities of brothers and sisters who feast at the table of Christ's sufficiency? What if these churches were known as communities of contentment and compassion? What if they were gossiped about, admired, beleaguered by curious inquirers? Such churches, having learned from the past, would have something authentic to contribute to the future.

# Notes

## Introduction

1. This definition of conversion—a change of belief, behavior, and belonging, accompanied by experience—is my own. For the alliteration I am indebted to Grace Davie, *Religion in Britain Since 1945: Believing Without Belonging* (Davie 1994). The categories are similar to those of Eugene V. Gallagher, who—without alliteration—wrote of "the cosmic, moral and social dimensions of Christian conversion" (1990:120).

## Chapter 1:
## The Conversions of Justin and Cyprian

1. Editions used: *Apology*, by E. R. Hardy, in C. C. Richardson 1970; *Apology* and *Dialogue with Trypho*, in Ante-Nicene Fathers (ANF) 1; *Acts of Justin*, in Musurillo 1972.

2. For what follows, see Justin, *Dialogue with Trypho* 2–8. Scholars debate the historicity of this account and the extent to which it can be harmonized with another account in Justin's *2 Apol* 12; for a discussion, see Skarsaune 1976:30. Henry Chadwick (1965:286) sees Justin's autobiography as "essentially veracious.... Like the rest of us, Justin is remembering the past in a way that the present requires."

3. For a model of conversion similar to Justin's, see Taber 1987.

4. Edition used: ANF 5.

5. The main sources for Cyprian's conversion are his own letter, *Ad Donatum*, and Pontius's *Vita Cypriani*. Maurice Wiles has challenged the authenticity of the former account; in it he does not detect "the personal anguish of soul" that he would expect in a conversion account (1963:140–41). I find, in contrast, that the insights gained through the struggle with the addictive powers of wealth that Cyprian reports permeate his writings; he obviously thought deeply and existentially about this issue (see, for example, *De Opere et Eleemosynis; Ad Quirinum* 3.1). And I agree with Elisabeth Fink-Dendorfer (1986:40), who detects "deeply felt spiritual strife" in *Ad Donatum* 3–4.

## Chapter 2:
### The Intriguing Attraction of Early Christianity

1. Editions used: Minucius Felix, *Octavius*, ed. G. H. Rendell, in Loeb Classical Library 250; Tertullian, *To His Wife,* in ANF 4; *Passio Perpetuae*, in Musurillo 1972:107ff; *Testamentum Domini,* ed. Cooper and MacLean 1902; *Didascalia Apostolorum*, ed. Connolly 1929; 2 Clement, ed. C. C. Richardson, and *Epistle to Diognetus,* ed. E. H. Fairweather, both in Richardson 1970; *Apostolic Tradition*, in Cuming 1987; Cyprian and Pontius, in ANF 5; Origen, *Contra Celsum* (Chadwick 1953); Origen, *Hom on Sam*, in Nautin and Nautin 1986; Irenaeus, in ANF 1; *First Greek Life of Pachomius*, in Veilleux 1980; *Canons of Hippolytus*, ed. Bradshaw 1987.

2. For other accounts, see Minucius Felix, *Octavius* 27.5; Tertullian, *Ad Scapulam* 2; Justin, 2 Apol 6.

## Chapter 3:
### The Journey of Conversion

1. Editions used: Tertullian, *On Baptism*, in ANF 3; *Apostolic Tradition*, in Cuming 1987; Cyprian and Pontius, in ANF 5; Origen, in ANF 4, except for *Contra Celsum* (Chadwick 1953), *Hom on Joshua* (Joubert 1960), and *Hom*

*on Luke* (Périchon 1962); Aristeides, *Apology*, in Stevenson 1987; Athenagoras, in Richardson 1970; Gregory of Pontus (Thaumaturgus), in ANF 6; *Canons of Elvira*, in Laeuchli 1972.

2. One must alas use quotation marks for this "document" because, strictly speaking, it does not exist. It is a cluster of parallel documents in various languages that scholars earlier in the twentieth century have melded into a single "reconstituted" document and attributed to Hippolytus of Rome (Dix 1968; Cuming 1987, which I use). Experts now see this solution as too simple, and are working to establish better texts and to discern probable dates and authorship (Bradshaw 1996). Until they do so, for our study of conversion we can draw upon a cluster of texts, probably of Roman origin but incorporating North Africa materials, that survive in Arabic, Ethiopic, and Sahidic (Coptic) translations.

3. A hint of the content of catechesis during Stage 3 is given by *Ap Trad* 21: "You have already been instructed about the resurrection of the flesh..."

4. In the fourth century a number of catechists gave considerable elaboration to these postbaptismal instructions, which liturgical scholars have labeled "mystagogy"—Stage 4 of the conversion process.

5. For example: Justin, *Dialogue with Trypho* 109, 1 *Apol* 39; Irenaeus, *Adversus Haereses* 4.34.4; Tertullian, *Adv Marc* 3.21, *Answer to the Jews* 3; Origen, *Contra Celsum* 5.33; *Didascalia Apostolorum* 6.5; Firmilian, Letter to Cyprian (Cyprian, *Ep* 74[75].1); Lactantius, *Div Inst* 4.17; Athanasius, *On the Incarnation* 52.

6. Tertullian, *De Patientia* 6; Clement of Alexandria, *Protrepticus* 10; Origen, *Contra Celsum* 3.8, 10; *Didascalia Apostolorum* 6.23.

### Chapter 4:
### Constantine Broadens the Attraction

1. There are two accounts of Constantine's visions of 312. I have relied on Lactantius, *De Mort Pers* 44.4–6; but see also the later, and more elaborate, account in Eusebius, *Vita Constantini (VC)* 1.29–31.

2. Editions used: Lactantius, in ANF 7; Eusebius, *Vita Constantini*, in Nicene and Post-Nicene Fathers (NPNF), 2d ser., 1 (except for *VC* 4.61–64, for which I have used Yarnold 1993:95–96); *Acts of Phileas*, in MacMullen and Lane 1992; *Apostolic Constitutions*, ed. Donaldson 1886; Augustine, *Confessions*, in Chadwick 1991; Gregory of Nazianzus, *Oratio* 40, in NPNF, 2d ser., 7.

3. For the date of the *Oration*, see Lane Fox 1986:643.

4. I have used the translation of this text by E. J. Yarnold 1993:95–96, and also am largely in agreement with his interpretation of the event.

5. After Constantine's death, purple reasserted its place in imperial symbolism: Constantine's casket was draped in purple cloth, and subsequent emperors wore purple. Significantly, before long purple was also adopted as an attire of the upper clergy (Eusebius, *VC* 4.66; Reinhold 1970:62, 68, 130).

6. Outbreaks of miracles continued to be attested to in missionary situations on the frontiers, e.g., the ministry of Martin of Tours in Gaul (Sulpicius Severus, *Dial* 2.5).

7. Talley 1991:203f; John Chrysostom, *Baptismal Instructions* 9.29; Leo the Great, *Sermons* 58.1; Egeria, *Travels* 46.1.

8. For other appeals to catechumens to present themselves for catechism study and baptism, see Ambrose, *De Elia et Ieiunio*; Augustine, *Sermon* 40.5; Caesarius of Arles, *Sermon* 200.

9. This could involve bishops, such as Hilary of Poitiers, or ascetic leaders such as Eustathius of Sebaste. See Klauser 1962:172–74; Rousseau 1994:74–75.

### Chapter 5:
### Catechizing the Masses: Cyril and Chrysostom

1. Editions used: Egeria, *Travels*, in Wilkinson 1981; Cyril, *Catechetical Lectures*, in NPNF, 2d ser., 7; John Chrysostom, *Baptismal Instructions*, in Harkins 1963; Ambrose, *De Mysteriis*, in Srawley 1919.

2. Ferguson forthcoming surveys the debate concerning whether the five mystagogic lectures were given by Cyril or by his successor, John.

3. Chrysostom dealt with the Isaiah 2/Micah 4 passages in his *Commentary on Isaiah* 2.2–5.

## Chapter 6:
### Attracting the Recalcitrant: Augustine and Volusian

1. Sources used: Augustine, *Confessions*, in Chadwick 1991; *Sermons*, in Hill 1990–1993; *First Catechetical Instruction*, in Christopher 1952; *On Faith and Works*, in Lombardo 1988; Gerontius, *Life of Melania the Younger*, in Clark 1984; *Ep* 93 and 135–38, in Parsons 1953 and Parsons 1953a; *Retractions*, in Bogan 1968.

2. The Fourth Council of Carthage changed the church's policy about admitting outsiders to its worship: canon 84 stipulated that "the bishop shall not forbid to anyone, whether pagan, heretic or Jew, entry into the church, and shall not prevent them from hearing the Word of God up to the moment of the mass of the catechumens." The date of this is uncertain, but it is clearly far later than the year 398 to which it has customarily been dated, and also, it seems to me, much later than Augustine's era. See Hefele 1908:2, i, 102.

3. Augustine's conversation with a would–be catechumen concentrated on motivation (Harmless 1995:113); two centuries earlier the catechists in the *Apostolic Tradition* (15–16) inquired into the candidates' relationships, jobs, and lifestyles.

4. "Augustine did not cite Isaiah 2:4 and its Micah parallel even a single time" (Lohfink 1986:202). In his *Confessions* (9.5) he reports that when he, prior to his final baptismal preparations, had asked Ambrose for a suitable reading, Ambrose proposed "the prophet Isaiah"; but Augustine found the early part of Isaiah difficult to understand, so he put the book aside (Harmless 1995:93).

5. Material on Volusian's family and career have been collected in Chastagnol 1956; see also Chastagnol 1962; Clark 1984:129–33.

## Chapter 7:
### Converting the Christians: Caearius of Arles

1. Sources used: Caesarius, *Sermons*, in Mueller 1956–1973; *Sermon* 54, in Klingshirn 1994:239; *Statuta*

*sanctarum virginum*, in de Vogüé 1988; *Vita Caesarii*, in Klingshirn 1994a; Cassian, *Conferences*, in NPNF, 2d ser., 11; Gregory Nazianzus, *Oratio* 40, in NPNF, 2d ser., 7.

2. Tithing was a practice notable for its absence in pre-Christendom Christianity. In the West it made its entry as a compulsory practice—a kind of Christendom tax—with the second council of Mâcon (585), canon 5. See Gaudemet and Basdevant 1989:2.462; Vischer 1966; Kreider 1995:43n.

3. An outstanding example of a church historian learning from missiologists, from whom I have profited much, is Russell 1994.

### Chapter 8:
### Christendom—Product of Conversion—
### and Some Clues About the Future of Christianity

1. Judith Herrin 1987 similarly does not define Christendom. But on page 479, in a passage dealing with the crumbling of Christendom, she lists two of its essential components: "the dominance of religion" and an absence of "choice."

2. Sources used: Gregory of Tours, *History of the Franks* 2.31, with significant details provided by Avitus of Vienne's letter to Clovis (c. 496), in Hillgarth 1986:77.

3. This is the likely meaning of the slightly ambiguous Latin text: "cum sub casside crinis nutritus salutarem galeam sacrae unctionis indueret" (Peiper 1883:75). I am grateful to Dr. Mark Atherton for discussing the problems of translating the text.

4. Sources used: Gregory of Tours, *History of the Franks* 5.11, with elaborations from Venantius Fortunatus, *Carmen* 5.5. For comment, see Reydellet 1992 and Goffart 1985.

5. For another list of Christendom's characteristics, see "The Constantinian Sources of Western Social Ethics," in Yoder 1984:135–41.

6. Butterfield 1949:136; Salzman 1993:378; MacMullen 1984:119. See also Kahl 1978:42, who speaks of "direkter Zwang und indirekte Nötigung."

7. I owe this information to Sir John Houghton.

# References Cited

Abraham, William J. 1989. *The Logic of Evangelism*. London: Hodder & Stoughton.

Aland, Kurt. 1961. *Über den Glaubenswechsel in der Geschichte des Christentums*. Berlin: Töpelmann.

Bardy, Gustave. 1949. *La Conversion au christianisme durant les premiers siècles*. Paris: Aubier.

Barnes, Timothy D. 1981. *Constantine and Eusebius*. Cambridge: Harvard University Press.

——. 1985. The Conversion of Constantine. *Classical Views* n.s. 4:371–91.

Batiffol, Pierre. 1913. Les Étapes de la conversion de Constantin. *Bulletin d'ancienne littérature et d'archéologie chrétienne* 3:178–88, 241–64.

Beck, Henry G. J. 1950. *The Pastoral Care of Souls in South-East France during the Sixth Century*. Analecta Gregoriana, 51. Rome: Pontifical Gregorian University.

Belche, Jean-Pierre. 1977. Die Bekehrung zum Christentum nach Augustins Büchlein De Catechizandis Rudibus. *Augustiniana* 27:26–69.

Bogan, Mary Inez, ed. 1968. *Saint Augustine: The Retractions*. The Fathers of the Church, 60. Washington, D.C.: Catholic University of America Press.

Bolt, John, and Richard A. Muller. 1996. Does the Church Today Need a New "Mission Paradigm"? *Calvin Theological Journal* 31:196–208.

Bradshaw, Paul F., ed. 1987. *The Canons of Hippolytus.* Alcuin/GROW Liturgical Study 2. Bramcote, Nottingham: Grove Books.

——. 1996. Redating the Apostolic Tradition: Some Preliminary Steps. In Nathan Mitchell and John F. Baldovin, eds., *Rule of Prayer, Rule of Faith: Essays in Honor of Aidan Kavenagh, O.S.B.* Collegeville: Liturgical Press, 3–17.

——. forthcoming. The Effects of the Coming of Christendom on Early Christian Worship. In Alan Kreider, ed., *The Origins of Christendom in the West* (forthcoming).

Brown, Peter. 1972. Aspects of the Christianization of the Roman Aristocracy. In his *Religion and Society in the Age of St. Augustine.* New York: Harper & Row, 161–82.

——. 1989. *The Body and Society: Men, Women and Sexual Renunciation in Early Christianity.* London: Faber & Faber.

——. 1996. *The Rise of Western Christendom: Triumph and Diversity, AD 200–1000.* Oxford: Blackwell.

Brueggemann, Walter. 1997. *Theology of the Old Testament: Testimony, Dispute, Advocacy.* Minneapolis: Fortress Press.

Burckhardt, Jakob. 1956. *The Age of Constantine the Great.* Garden City, N.Y.: Doubleday Anchor Books.

Butterfield, Herbert. 1949. *Christianity and History.* New York: Charles Scribner's Sons.

Chadwick, Henry, ed. 1953. *Origen: Contra Celsum.* Cambridge: Cambridge University Press.

——. 1965. Justin Martyr's Defence of Christianity. *Bulletin of the John Rylands Library* 47:275–97.

——, ed. 1991. *Saint Augustine Confessions.* Oxford: Oxford University Press.

*Challenge.* 1983. *The Challenge of Peace.* The U.S. Roman Catholic Bishops' Pastoral Letter on War and Peace. London: Catholic Truth Society.

Chastagnol, André. 1956. Le Sénateur Volusien et la conversion d'une famille de l'aristocratie romaine au bas-empire. *Revue des études anciennes* 58: 241–53.

——. 1962. *Les Fastes de la Préfecture de Rome au Bas-Empire.* Études Prosopographiques, 2. Paris: Nouvelles Éditions Latines.

Christopher, J. P., ed. 1952. *St. Augustine: The First Catechetical Instruction.* Ancient Christian Writers, 2. Westminster, Md.: Newman Press.

Chupungco, Anscar J. 1989. *Liturgies of the Future.* New York: Paulist Press.

Clark, Elizabeth A., ed. 1984. *The Life of Melania the Younger.* Studies in Women and Religion, 14. Lewiston, N.Y.: Edwin Mellen Press.

Coleman-Norton, P. R., ed. 1966. Roman State and Christian Church: A Collection of Legal Documents to A.D. 535. 3 vols. London: SPCK.

Connolly, R. Hugh, ed. 1929. *Didascalia Apostolorum.* Oxford: Clarendon Press.

Cooper, James, and A. J. MacLean, eds. 1902. *Testamentum Domini.* Edinburgh: T. & T. Clark.

Cuming, Geoffrey J., ed. 1987. *Hippolytus: A Text for Students.* 2d ed. Bramcote, Nottingham: Grove Books.

Davie, Grace. 1994. *Religion in Britain Since 1945: Believing Without Belonging.* Oxford: Blackwell.

Deléani, Simone. 1979. *Christum sequi: Étude d'un theme dans l'oeuvre de saint Cyprien.* Paris: Études Augustiniennes.

Didier, J.-Ch. 1965. Une Adaptation de la liturgie baptismale au baptême des enfants dans l'Église ancienne. *Melanges de science religieuse* 22 (1965):79–90.

Dix, Gregory. 1968. *The Apostolic Tradition of St. Hippolytus.* 2d ed., rev. Henry Chadwick. London: SPCK.

Donaldson, James, ed. 1886. *Constitutions of the Holy Apostles.* Edinburgh.

Ellul, Jacques. 1986. *The Subversion of Christianity.* Grand Rapids: Eerdmans.

Engelmann, Ursmar. 1959. *Der heilige Pirmin und sein Missionsbüchlein*. Konstanz: Jan Thorbecke Verlag.

Ferguson, Everett. 1979. Inscriptions and the Origin of Infant Baptism. *Journal of Theological Studies* n.s. 30:37–46.

———. 1984. *Demonology of the Early Christian World*. Symposium Series, 12. New York: Edwin Mellen Press.

———. 1989. Irenaeus' Proof of the Apostolic Preaching and Early Catechetical Tradition. *Studia Patristica* 18. 3(1989):119–40.

———. forthcoming. Catechesis and Initiation. In Alan Kreider, ed., *The Origins of Christendom in the West* (forthcoming).

Field, Anne. 1997. *From Darkness to Light: How One Became a Christian in the Early Church*. Ben Lomond, Calif.: Conciliar Press.

Fink-Dendorfer, Elisabeth. 1986. *Conversio: Motive und Motivierung zur Bekehrung in der Alten Kirche*. Regensburger Studien zur Theologie, 33. Frankfurt-am-Main: Verlag Peter Lang.

Finn, Thomas M. 1990. It Happened One Saturday Night: Ritual and Conversion in Augustine's North Africa. *Journal of the American Academy of Religion* 58/4:589–616.

———. 1997. *From Death to Rebirth: Ritual and Conversion in Antiquity*. Mahwah, N.J.: Paulist Press.

Fisher, J. D. C., and E. J. Yarnold. 1992. The West from about A.D. 500 to the Reformation. In Cheslyn Jones et al., eds., *The Study of Liturgy*. Rev ed. London: SPCK.

Fontaine, Jacques. 1972. Valeurs antiques et valeurs chrétiennes dans la spiritualité des grands propriétaires terriens à la fin du IVe siècle occidental. In *Epektasis: Mélanges patristiques offerts au Cardinal Jean Daniélou*. Paris: Beauchesne, 571–95.

Fouracre, Paul. 1979. The Work of Audoenus of Rouen and Eligius of Noyon in Extending Episcopal Influence from the Town to the Country in Seventh-Century Neustria. In Derek Baker, ed., *The Church in Town and*

*Countryside*. Studies in Church History,16. Oxford: Basil Blackwell, 77–91.

Gallagher, Eugene V. 1990. *Expectation and Experience: Explaining Religious Conversion*. Atlanta: Scholars Press.

Gaudemet, Jean. 1958. *L'Église dans l'Empire Romain (IVᵉ–Vᵉ siècles)*. Vol. 3. *Histoire du Droit et des Institutions de l'Église en Occident*. Paris: Sirey.

——, and Brigitte Basdevant, eds. 1989. *Les Canons des conciles Mérovingiens* (VIᵉ–VIIᵉ siècles). 2 vols. Sources chrétiennes, 353–54. Paris: Cerf.

Geerlings, W. 1987. Bekehrung durch Belehrung: Zur 1600. Jahresfeier der Bekehrung Augustins. *Theologische Quartalschrift* 167 (1987):195–208.

Goffart, Walter. 1985. The Conversions of Avitus of Clermont, and Similar Passages in Gregory of Tours. In J. Neusner and E. S. Frerichs, eds., *"To See Others as Others See Us": Christians, Jews, "Others" in Late Antiquity*. Chico, Calif.: Scholars Press, 473–97.

Hamman, Adalbert. 1992. Catechumen, Catechumenate. In *Encyclopedia of the Early Church*, ed. Angelo di Berardino, I. Cambridge: James Clarke, 151–52.

Harkins, Paul W., ed. 1963. *St. John Chrysostom: Baptismal Instructions*. Ancient Christian Writers, 31. Westminster, Md.: Newman Press.

Harmless, William. 1995. *Augustine and the Catechumenate*. Collegeville: Liturgical Press.

Hauerwas, Stanley. 1991. *After Christendom*. Nashville: Abingdon Press.

Hauerwas, Stanley, and William H. Willimon. 1989. *Resident Aliens*. Nashville: Abingdon Press.

Hefele, Joseph. 1908. *Histoire des Conciles*. Vol. 2, i. Paris: Letouzey et Ané.

Herrin, Judith. 1987. *The Formation of Christendom*. Princeton: Princeton University Press.

Hill, Edmund, ed. 1990–1993. *Saint Augustine, Sermons*. The Works of Saint Augustine, III/1–6. New York and New Rochelle, NY: New City Press.

Hillgarth, J. N., ed. 1986. *Christianity and Paganism, 350–750.* Philadelphia: University of Pennsylvania Press.

Hornus, Jean-Michel. 1980. *It Is Not Lawful for Me to Fight: Early Christian Attitudes Toward War, Violence and the State.* Rev. ed. Scottdale, Pa.: Herald Press.

Jegen, M. E. 1967. Catechesis II (Medieval and Modern). In *New Catholic Encyclopedia*, 3. New York: McGraw-Hill, 209–215.

Jones, Prudence, and Nigel Pennick. 1995. *A History of Pagan Europe.* London: Routledge.

Joubert, Annie, ed. 1960. *Origène, Homélies sur Josué.* Sources chrétiennes, 71. Paris: Cerf.

Judge, E. A. 1977. The Earliest Use of Monachos for "Monk" (P. Coll. Youtie 77) and the Origins of Monasticism. *Jahrbuch für Antike und Christentum* 20:72–89.

Kahl, Hans-Dietrich. 1978. Die ersten Jahrhunderte des missiongeschichtlichen Mittelalters. In Knut Schäferdiek, ed., *Kirchengeschichte als Missionsgeschichte*, IIa, *Die Kirche des frühen Mittelalters.* Munich: Chr. Kaiser, 11–76.

Kee, Alastair. 1982. *Constantine Versus Christ: The Triumph of Ideology.* London: SCM Press.

Khatchatrian, A. 1982. *Origine et typologie des baptistères paléochrétiens.* Mulhouse: Centre de culture chrétienne.

Klauser, Theodor. 1962. Bischöfe auf dem Richterstuhl. *Jahrbuch für Antike und Christentum* 5:172–74.

Klingshirn, William E. 1994. *Caesarius of Arles: The Making of a Christian Community in Late Antique Gaul.* Cambridge: Cambridge University Press.

——, ed. 1994a. *Caesarius of Arles: Life, Testament, Letters.* Translated Texts for Historians, 19. Liverpool: Liverpool University Press.

Kreider, Alan. 1995. *Worship and Evangelism in Pre-Christendom.* Alcuin/GROW Liturgical Study 32. Cambridge: Grove Books.

——. 1996. Baptism, Catechism, and the Eclipse of Jesus' Teaching in Early Christianity. *Tyndale Bulletin* 47/2:315–48.

——. 1997. Oaths. In Everett Ferguson, ed., *Encyclopedia of Early Christianity*, 2. New York: Garland Publishing, 823–24.

Labriolle, Pierre de. 1927. Paroecia. *Bulletin du Cange (Archivum Latinitatis Medii Aevi)* 3:196–207.

Laeuchli, Samuel. 1972. *Power and Sexuality*. Philadelphia: Temple University Press.

Lane Fox, Robin. 1986. *Pagans and Christians*. San Francisco: Harper & Row.

Latourette, Kenneth Scott. 1944. *A History of the Expansion of Christianity*. I: *The First Five Centuries*. London: Eyre and Spottiswoode.

Lepelley, Claude. 1979. *Les Cités de l'Afrique Romaine au Bas-Empire*, I. Paris: Études Augustiniennes.

——. 1984. Chrétiens et paiens au temps de la persécution de Dioclétien: le cas d'Abthungi. *Studia Patristica* 15:226–32.

Lizzi, Rita. 1990. Ambrose's Contemporaries and the Christianization of Northern Italy. *Journal of Roman Studies* 80: 156–73.

Lohfink, Gerhard. 1986. 'Schwertzer zu Pflugscharen': Die Rezeption von Jes 2, 1–5 par Mi 4, 1–5 in der Alten Kirche und im Neuen Testament. *Theologische Quartalschrift* 166:184–209.

Lombardo, Gregory J., ed. 1988. *St Augustine: On Faith and Works*. Ancient Christian Writers, 48. New York: Newman Press.

Lynch, Joseph H. 1986. *Godparents and Kinship in Early Medieval Europe*. Princeton: Princeton University Press.

MacDonald, Margaret Y. 1996. *Early Christian Women and Pagan Opinion: The Power of the Hysterical Woman*. Cambridge: Cambridge University Press.

MacMullen, Ramsay. 1969. *Constantine*. London: Croom Helm.

——. 1983. Two Types of Conversion to Early Christianity. *Vigiliae Christianae* 37: 174–92.

——. 1984. *Christianizing the Roman Empire (A.D. 100–400)*. New Haven: Yale University Press.

——. 1988. *Corruption and the Decline of Rome*. New Haven: Yale University Press.

——. 1990. Judicial Savagery in the Roman Empire. In his *Changes in the Roman Empire: Essays in the Ordinary.* Princeton: Princeton University Press, 204–17.

——. 1997. *Christianity and Paganism in the Fourth to Eighth Centuries*. New Haven: Yale University Press.

——, and Eugene N. Lane, eds. 1992. *Paganism and Christianity, 100–425 C.E.: A Sourcebook*. Minneapolis: Fortress Press.

Madec, Goulven. 1986. Conuersio. In Cornelius Meyer, ed., *Augustinus Lexikon*, 1. Basel: Schwabe.

Malone, Edward E. 1951. Martyrdom and Monastic Profession as a Second Baptism. In A. Mayr, J. Quasten, and B. Neunheuser, eds., *Vom Christlichen Mysterium: Gesammelte Arbeiten zum Gedächtnis von Odo Casel OSB*. Düsseldorf: Patmos Verlag, 115-34.

Meeks, Wayne A. 1993. *The Origins of Christian Morality: The First Two Centuries*. New Haven: Yale University Press.

Meeks, Wayne A., and Robert L. Wilken. 1978. *Jews and Christians in Antioch in the First Four Centuries of the Common Era*. Society of Biblical Literature, Sources for Biblical Study, 13. Missoula, Mont.: Scholars Press, 1978.

Miles, Margaret R. 1989. *Carnal Knowing: Female Nakedness and Religious Meaning in the Christian West*. Boston: Beacon Press.

Mitchell, Stephen. 1993. *Anatolia: Land, Men, and Gods in Asia Minor.* II: *The Rise of the Church*. Oxford: Clarendon Press.

Mohrmann, Christine. 1961. *Études sur le Latin des Chrétiens*, 2. Rome: Edizioni di Storia et Letteratura.

Moorhead, John. 1985. Clovis' Motives for Becoming a Catholic Christian. *Journal of Religious History* 13:329–39.

Mueller, Mary Magdaleine. ed. 1956–1973. *Saint Caesarius of Arles: Sermons*. 3 vols. The Fathers of the Church, 31, 47, 66. Washington, D.C.: Catholic University of America Press.

Musurillo, Herbert, ed. 1972. *The Acts of the Christian Martyrs*. Oxford: Clarendon Press.

Myers, Norman. 1997. Consumption in Relation to Population, Environment and Development. *The Environmentalist* 17:33–44.

Nautin, Pierre, and Marie-Thérèse Nautin, eds. 1986. *Origène, Homélies sur Samuel*. Sources chrétiennes, 328. Paris: Cerf.

Nock, Arthur Darby. 1933. *Conversion*. Oxford: Clarendon Press.

O'Donovan, Oliver. 1996. *The Desire of the Nations: Rediscovering the Roots of Political Theology*. Cambridge: Cambridge University Press.

Parsons, Wilfrid, ed. 1953. *Saint Augustine, Letters, II (83–130)*. The Fathers of the Church, 18. Washington, D.C.: Catholic University of America Press.

——, ed. 1953a. *Saint Augustine, Letters III (131–164)*. The Fathers of the Church, 20. Washington, D.C.: Catholic University of America Press.

Peiper, Rudolf. 1883. *Alcimi Ecdicii Aviti Viennensis Episcopi Opera*. MGH AA VI.2. Berlin: Weidmann.

Périchon, Pierre, ed. 1962. *Origène, Homélies sur S. Luc*. Sources chrétiennes, 87. Paris: Cerf.

Pharr, Clyde, ed. 1952. *The Theodosian Code and Novels and the Sirmondian Constitutions*. Princeton: Princeton University Press.

Piédagnel, Auguste, ed. 1990. *Jean Chrysostome: Trois catechèses baptismales*. Sources chrétiennes, 366. Paris: Cerf.

Poque, Suzanne, ed. 1966. *Augustin d'Hippone: Sermons pour la Pâque*. Sources chrétiennes, 116. Paris: Cerf.

Quacquarelli, Antonio. 1971. Note retoriche sui *Testimonia* di Cipriano. *Vetera Christianorum* 8:181–209.

Reinhold, Meyer. 1970. *History of Purple as a Status Symbol in Late Antiquity*. Collection Latomus, 116. Brussels: Latomus.

Reydellet, Marc. 1992. La conversion des Juifs de Clermont en 576. In Louis Holtz and Jean-Claude Fredouille, eds.,

*De Tertullien aux Mozarabes* (FS J. Fontaine). Paris: Études Augustiniennes: I, 371–79.

Richardson, C. C., ed. 1970. *Early Christian Fathers*. New York: Macmillan.

Rohr, Richard. 1991. *Simplicity: The Art of Living*. New York: Crossroad.

Rousseau, Philip. 1994. *Basil of Caesarea*. Berkeley: University of California Press.

Russell, James C. 1994. *The Germanization of Early Medieval Christianity: A Sociohistorical Approach to Religious Transformation*. New York: Oxford University Press.

Salzman, Michelle Renee. 1993. The Evidence for the Conversion of the Roman Empire to Christianity in Book 16 of the *Theodosian Code*. *Historia* 42:362–78.

Skarsaune, Oscar. 1976. The Conversion of Justin Martyr. *Studia Theologica* (Oslo) 30:53–73.

Snyder, Graydon F. 1985. *Ante Pacem: Archaeological Evidence of Church Life Before Constantine*. Macon, Ga.: Mercer University Press.

Srawley, J. H. 1919. *St. Ambrose, On the Mysteries*. London, SPCK.

Stancliffe, C. E. 1979. From Town to Country: The Christianisation of the Touraine, 370–600. In Derek Baker, ed., *The Church in Town and Countryside.* Studies in Church History, 16. Oxford: Basil Blackwell, 43–59.

Stark, Rodney. 1996. *Reconstructing the Rise of Christianity: Adventures in Historical Sociology*. Princeton: Princeton Unversity Press.

Stauffer, S. Anita. 1994. *On Baptismal Fonts: Ancient and Modern.* Alcuin/GROW Liturgical Study 29–30. Bramcote, Nottingham: Grove Books.

Stevenson, J., ed. 1987. *A New Eusebius: Documents illustrating the History of the Church to A.D. 337*. Ed. W. H. C. Frend. London: SPCK.

Taber, Charles R. 1987. God vs. Idols: A Model of Conversion. *Journal of the Academy for Evangelism in Theological Education* 3:20–32.

Talley, Thomas J. 1991. *The Origins of the Liturgical Year.* Collegeville, Minn.: Liturgical Press.

Thompson, E. A. 1960. The Conversion of the Visigoths to Catholicism. *Nottingham Medieval Studies* 4:4–35.

Tippett, Alan R., Tetsunao Yamamori, and Charles R. Taber. 1975. *Christopaganism or Indigenous Christianity?* Pasadena, Calif.: William Carey Library.

Van der Meer, F. 1961. *Augustine the Bishop: The Life and Work of a Father of the Church.* London: Sheed & Ward.

Van Engen, John. 1986. The Christian Middle Ages as An Historiographical Problem. *American Historical Review* 91:519–52.

Veilleux, Armand, ed. 1980. *Pachomian Koinonia.* I: *The Life of Saint Pachomius and His Disciples.* Kalamazoo, Mich.: Cistercian Publications.

Vischer, Lukas. 1966. *Tithing in the Early Church.* Philadelphia: Fortress Press.

Vogüé, A. de, and J. Courreau, eds. 1988. *Césaire d'Arles, Œuvres Monastiques* I. Sources chrétiennes, 345. Paris: Cerf.

Wessels, Anton. 1994. *Europe: Was It Ever Really Christian? The Interaction Between Gospel and Culture.* London: SCM Press.

Westerhoff, John H. 1992. Fashioning Christians in Our Day. In Stanley Hauerwas and John H. Westerhoff, eds., *Schooling Christians: "Holy Experiments" in American Education.* Grand Rapids: Eerdmans, 262–81.

Whitaker, E. C., ed. 1970. *Documents of the Baptismal Liturgy.* Rev. ed. London: SPCK.

Wiles, Maurice F. 1963. The Theological Legacy of St Cyprian. *Journal of Ecclesiastical History* 14:139–49.

Wilken, Robert L. 1984. *The Christians as the Romans Saw Them.* New Haven: Yale University Press.

——. 1995. *Remembering the Christian Past.* Grand Rapids: Eerdmans, 1995.

Wilkinson, John, ed. 1981. *Egeria's Travels to the Holy Land.* Rev. ed. Jerusalem: Ariel.

Wischmeyer, Wolfgang. 1992. *Von Golgatha zum Ponte Molle: Studien zur Sozialgeschichte der Kirche im dritten Jahrhundert.* Forschungen zur Kirchen- und Dogmengeschichte, 49. Göttingen: Vandenhoeck & Ruprecht.

Wright, David F. 1987. The Origins of Infant Baptism—Child Believers' Baptism? *Scottish Journal of Theology* 40:1–23.

——. 1997. At What Ages Were People Baptized in the Early Centuries? *Studia Patristica* 30:389–94.

——. forthcoming. Augustine and the Transformation of Baptism. In Alan Kreider, ed., *The Origins of Christendom in the West* (forthcoming).

Yarnold, E. J. 1971. *The Awe-Inspiring Rites of Initiation.* Slough, England: St. Paul Publications.

——. 1993. The Baptism of Constantine. *Studia Patristica* 26:95–101.

Yoder, John Howard. 1984. *The Priestly Kingdom: Social Ethics as Gospel.* Notre Dame: University of Notre Dame Press.